To Paula Veloso Babadi, for believing in this
project

*Writing without revising is the literary equivalent
of waltzing gaily out of the house in your
underwear.*

–PATRICIA FULLER

The (Dubious) Joy of Editing

Sharpening Your Manuscript Without Dulling Your Voice

 The *Write Boost* Writing Series

Karina Fabian

Laser Cow Press

MERRITT ISLAND, FL

Laser Cow Press
Merritt Island, FL
https://fabianspace.com

Book Layout © 2017 BookDesignTemplates.com
Cover art by Karina Fabian using ChatGPT for the image
This book was made with the assistance of ChatGPT based on author speeches and notes and was extensively rewritten.

The (Dubious) Joy of Editing: Sharpening Your Manuscript Without Dulling Your Voice/ Karina Fabian -- 1st ed.
Print ISBN 978-1-956489-30-9

Contents

Editing Is Not for Wimps

Editing hurts.

Real editing isn't just a check for typos. It's going at your manuscript with a scalpel—or a machete—and carving out what doesn't work, then grafting in what does. It means taking a story you love and treating it with a cold eye.

What is strong? What is weak? What serves the story? Does that impressive section advance the story, or does it just make you look good?

It's where you admit that the clever subplot you adored doesn't actually serve the book. Where you realize your beloved character is a "Mary Sue."

Where you discover that the emergency you built an *entire opening chapter* around...would never happen.

Yep. I've done that.

When I was revising *Discovery*, I had to perform reconstructive surgery on the manuscript. I'd already been writing this book for seven years, but I was sure I'd gotten it. Now, I started with an opening chapter that was dramatic, tense, and a strong introduction to the world. Sister Ann's spacesuit malfunctioned and she suffered nitrogen narcosis, which let her say things her superior would rather not hear. It set the stage. It was clever. It was useful.

It was completely wrong.

First: The chapter was hard sci-fi, while the rest of the book was soft sci-fi.

Second, it was 6000 words long—longer than the other chapters in the book by far.

Third, it took place on an asteroid we never see or hear from again.

But worst of all: It was *scientifically inaccurate*. Spacesuit air isn't a nitrogen mix. It's pressurized oxygen.

That meant the entire premise of my emergency collapsed. After I had already rewritten the chapter once (and the entire book nearly seven times already).

But I rewrote it again because I loved this story and wanted it to work. This time, a jagged piece of broken station strut pierced her suit. She sealed the leak with the plasticine adhesive I'd invented for the story and waited, impaled but stubborn, until rescue arrived. The theology stayed. The tension improved.

And the science stopped embarrassing me.

Editing hurts, but done well, it makes the entire book stronger.

That's what this book is about: learning to look at our stories with a critical eye, apply the blade to cut out what doesn't work, and do the reconstructive surgery to make it the best it can be.

Oh, and we'll have some tips for catching typos and grammatical errors, too.

Why You'll See So Much of My Own Work

You will notice that many of the examples in this book come from my own novels, articles, and early drafts.

That's intentional.

I've seen my manuscripts through the entire process—from messy draft to editorial redlines to final publication. I know where they broke. I know where they bloated. I know where I tried to sneak in a beloved subplot that had nothing to do with the theme. I know where my son stopped me mid-read-aloud and said, "Mom, you've got too many minions," because I'd lost track of who was still in the room.

I'm not embarrassed by those mistakes (well, maybe a little at the time). They are part of growing a story and growing as a writer.

It might be easy to dissect a classic to see what works, but as the saying goes, we can learn from other people's mistakes—and if sharing my mistakes helps you, I'm glad to do it. So, when I show you a clumsy sentence, a passive construction, a wandering subplot, or a logical inconsistency, and how I fixed them, understand that I'm not pointing from a pedestal. I'm standing beside you with a red pen in my own hand.

On occasion, I may share a paragraph or two that from published authors that illustrates a point especially well.

This Is Not Just About Fiction

The principles in this book apply just as strongly to nonfiction as to fiction. Some of the components are different yet are nonetheless similar. Your business article may not have a plot, per se, but it still needs to follow a logical structure, for example.

Clean manuscripts matter just as much in nonfiction—arguably more. In fiction, readers will sometimes forgive a loose paragraph if the story grips them. In nonfiction, clarity *is* the grip. If your argument wanders or your examples multiply without discipline, you lose authority.

So as we move through content, sentence beauty, and copy edit, I will address both fiction and nonfiction wherever possible. The tools differ slightly. The principles do not.

The Order Matters

Running your manuscript through a spellcheck or a grammar program is helpful, but it is not editing. It is tidying the counters during a kitchen renovation—sometimes it helps control the chaos, but you'll have to do it again and again as changes are made.

Run spelling and grammar check as you like, but we're going to tackle editing in deliberate layers:

- **Content:** Does the book work?
- **Sentence beauty:** Do the sentences carry their weight?
- **Copy edit:** Is the language clean and consistent?

Then we'll talk about the Six-Step System, which shows you how to execute your editing passes efficiently. The Six Steps are powerful, but they are not the starting point. A backward read will not fix a wandering theme. A font change will not repair a broken structure.

First, we determine what to look for. Then we learn how to find it.

Editing Is an Act of Respect

Editing is not punishment for having written badly.

It's a necessity if you want to be traditionally published. As more and more people are submitting, it's becoming increasingly important to have an excellently edited manuscript to rise above the rabble. Further, some publishers are starting to require that manuscripts be edited before submission. Providing a good, clean, well-edited copy tells the publisher you respect their time.

If you're self-publishing, then editing is an act of respect for your reader.

When an editor once told me that I sent in "clean copy," I took that as one of the highest compliments of my career. Clean copy means the acquiring editor can focus on nuance and shine rather than reconstructive surgery. It means you've done your homework.

It also means you've learned to detach just enough from your own prose to see it clearly.

That's the skill we're building here.

In the next section, we'll begin with the most difficult pass of all: content. We'll ask what your book is actually about—and whether every scene, paragraph, or argument truly supports it.

Bring your red pen.

Reflection Questions

➤ How do you approach editing—as a drudgery or as an adventure?

➤ Have you ever discovered a major error only after you thought a manuscript was finished?

➤ Are you more likely to over-edit sentences before the structure is solid, or avoid deep edits because they feel overwhelming?

Exercise

1. Choose one completed draft—fiction or nonfiction.
2. Without opening the document, write the core of the project in one or two sentences.

   - **For fiction:** What is the story truly about beneath the events?
   - **For nonfiction:** What is the main argument or promise to the reader?

Now open the manuscript and skim the chapter titles or scene breaks. Do they all point toward that core? Don't fix anything yet. Just observe.

What Is Your Book About?

Is there any better feeling than completing a manuscript? You're in love with your characters, the plot leaves you heart-warmed and maybe a little teary, and you just want to live in that world. Or if it's nonfiction, there's a feeling of satisfaction in the knowledge that you've done something that could be important to other people. I love that feeling. It's what keeps me writing.

I want you to love your book. You should. It's amazing to have written something. I've heard that only 1% of people who want to write a book actually finish it.

But now, you have to enter the realm of cool calculation, distance, and less emotional thinking. I'll bet, however, you'll also find it a time of discovery and an opportunity to congratulate yourself on a great turn of phrase or a clever scene. Editing is not all drudgery, but it does require a more critical eye.

That begins with distance.

Step One: Put Your Manuscript Away

I'll be honest. I'm awful at this part—and I pay for it. When you finish a book is generally not the best time to jump right into editing. You're too close to the plot, the characters, that metaphor you spent an hour in the shower coming up with, the amazing facts you discovered...

I get excited and I just want to jump in and start reading from the start.

However, editing when you are so close to the story does not give your brain time to reset. It will fill in things that aren't there—whether ignoring a skipped word because it knows it should be there or not realizing an analogy doesn't work because—*Oo! Exciting scene coming next!* That's why putting it away for a while helps.

Everyone has their own time frame. I've heard people say at least a month. Others a week. I often go back after a day, but I do admit that might be too soon.

Don't waste that time, however. Use it to:

- Recharge by doing some other creative work (or cleaning house).
- Create supporting matter for the story— back cover summaries, social media content, a first draft at a query letter...
- Write something else entirely.
- Start the next book.
- Read! Authors improve by reading other authors.

The Heart of Your Book

Before you sharpen sentences, fix commas, or start hunting down stray adverbs, you need to answer one deceptively simple question:

What is the book about?

You'd think that'd be an easy question after writing 80,000 words. Of course, we know what our book is about...until we have to write a 150-word pitch. Then you have to really dig deep into the core of your story—not just what happens but *what it's all about*. Why should anyone care? What should the reader walk away with?

This is a vital step not just when selling the story but when editing it. Fiction or nonfiction, when you sit down to revise a manuscript, you must know exactly what the story—or the argument—is trying to accomplish.

Otherwise, you have no reliable way to judge what belongs and what does not.

Manuscripts can get messy during drafting. That's not a flaw; it's part of the creative process. Drafting is exploration. You chase ideas, discover characters, try out scenes and arguments to see which ones spark. By the time you reach the end of a first draft, you may have written many good pages that simply do not belong in the final version.

Editing is where you decide which parts truly serve the book.

Plot and Theme

In fiction, a book is usually about two things: the plot and the theme.

The plot describes what happens. The theme explains why it matters.

Take Ernest Hemingway's *The Old Man and the Sea*. The plot is straightforward: An aging fisherman hooks a marlin that pulls him far out to sea, and he struggles to bring the fish home. But the theme—what the story ultimately expresses—is something deeper: *A man can be destroyed but not defeated.*

Readers usually talk about the plot. They remember the struggle with the marlin, the sharks, the long journey back to shore. The theme works more quietly. It settles in the mind as the emotional truth behind the events.

When plot and theme reinforce each other, the story becomes memorable. When they drift apart, the manuscript begins to feel like a series of incidents rather than a unified narrative.

One of the most useful tricks evaluating this alignment, I learned from Holly Lisle: Drill your story down until you can express it in a single sentence. Then examine each scene and ask how it supports that sentence.

That question can be ruthless.

It forces you to confront the scenes you love but that have wandered away from the heart of the story.

Why Should the Reader Care?

My first DragonEye, PI, novel, *Magic, Mensa, and Mayhem*, was an adaptation of a serial story. Essentially my dragon Vern was babysitting the Faerie folk at a Mensa convention in Florida and having a really tough time dealing with all the cultural misunderstandings. It was full of silliness and action, and I was really proud of it.

I'd gone to visit my friend, author Ann Lewis, in New York, a fellow founder of the Catholic Writers Guild. She was and is a big fan of Vern and she'd beta read the novel. As we were driving to her house from the airport, she told me how much she enjoyed the book except for one thing: *I didn't have any reason to care if Vern succeeded or failed.*

No matter how fun a book may be, without stakes, there's no reason for the reader to keep turning pages. They need to be invested in the main character's success, which means there needs to be consequences if the hero fails. This is true in comedy as well as tragedy.

Consequences can be external or internal, but they need to matter. As it was in the draft of *MM&M*, for example, the only stake was Vern would be embarrassed, as would the Faerie realm. As we used to say in high school debate: *So What/Who Cares/No Impact.*

As you consider your story, ask yourself: What happens if there hadn't been a happily ever after? Would someone's life change significantly? Many lives?

Really, this is a question to ask in the plotting, but especially if you are a pantster (someone who "discovery writes" aka—writes by the seat of their pants) then you may not have as strong a consequence as you imagined. This is what happened with me.

If you find this was the case, then fixing it is in your best interests. This may require rebuilding the plot (the topic of another book). Sometimes, however, it can be as simple as finding the main conflict and asking, "What's the worst thing that can happen if the character fails?"

Vern's null state is misunderstood, (and he's very annoyed about it), so I needed external stakes. The main conflict was the elves posturing for a conflict, so what if they wanted to drag the state of Florida into it? It was just high enough to make failure matter and ridiculous enough to fit into the plot.

Magic, Mensa, and Mayhem was reviewed in *Publisher's Weekly*, won the Mensa Owl, and won the Indie Awards for best fantasy—but it probably would not have if I hadn't taken my friend's advice and given the reader a reason to care.

It's not enough for the reader to want the protagonist to win; they need a reason to worry about what happens if they fail.

Killing the Sacred Subplot

Have you had this experience?

You fall in love with a character or an idea, and before you know it, the manuscript has drifted into a fascinating side story that has nothing to do with the main narrative.

I call it the sacred subplot.

I ran headlong into this problem while writing my *Madness of Kanaan* trilogy. In the second book, I explored the failed romance of my main character, Joshua. I loved writing those scenes. They were emotional and complex, and they helped illustrate differences between alien and human relationships. The romance even had a legitimate connection to the larger story because Joshua's ex eventually reappeared with a clue that helped resolve the main conflict.

So, the subplot wasn't irrelevant. However, I'd spent far too much time exploring it. I had flashbacks and long conversations where I wandered deep into the emotional woods...all for a secondary character's relationship—one that had ended before the novel even began.

My publisher read the manuscript and gently pointed out the obvious: Joshua was stranded on an alien planet trying to survive a crisis. Was he really going to spend this much time brooding about an ex-girlfriend from a year and a half ago?

She was right.

Out came the machete.

Some of those scenes were beautifully written, but they did not support the central story. Once they were cut, the book became tighter and the main narrative gained strength.

What's interesting is that an agent read the unedited version and told me she didn't care about the rest of the story—she wanted me to scrap the main theme and just write the subplot. To do that, though, I'd be writing another book in a completely different genre. That alone should tell you how much the subplot didn't really fit.

This is one of the hard lessons of editing: a scene or subplot can be good and still be wrong for the book.

However, there's a silver lining—when a subplot captures your heart that strongly, it might be another book waiting for you to write it.

Starting Too Early

Another common issue appears at the beginning of manuscripts. Writers often start the story before the story actually begins.

This is sometimes called literary throat clearing. The writer is warming up—establishing setting, introducing characters, laying out background information. None of that is inherently bad, but it often delays the moment when something meaningful happens.

There's an old bit of advice in writing circles that says you can usually cut the first chapter of a novel and improve the book. I don't believe that rule is universally true, but it is worth asking the question. Does the story actually begin here, or am I simply clearing my throat before the action starts?

When editing, look carefully at the opening chapters and ask whether they contain a genuine turning point. If nothing changes—if the characters begin and end the chapter in essentially the same place as far as plot or theme are concerned—you may be starting too early.

For example, imagine a mystery novel that opens with five pages describing the detective's apartment and morning routine before the crime is even mentioned. The writing might be atmospheric and pleasant to read, but the story hasn't started yet. If the murder investigation begins on page six, the manuscript may benefit from beginning on page six as well.

Now, don't get me wrong. Not every mystery has to start with a murder or the heist. A certain amount of scene-setting orients the reader. Sometimes, it's expected by genre.

You can still include the important background information. You simply distribute it more strategically throughout the narrative.

Remember the first chapter of *Discovery* that I told you about in the introduction? At the end of the day, it was 6000 words of literary throat clearing. I couldn't just cut it and start with Chapter Two, however. I had to find the proper start of the story. However, I have known others who were able to remove Chapter One and start with only a few additions to Chapter Two.

How do you know if you're starting the story in the correct spot? Ask yourself these questions:

- If I cut this chapter, how much information does the reader need right now to be able to move on?
- Does the character start on their hero's journey in this chapter? At what point?
- If you've already set the book aside and are coming in fresh, start by reading Chapter Two. How confused are you? How much does it depend on information from Chapter One?

Supporting the Theme

Scenes that do belong in the story should still be evaluated for how well they support the theme.

This does not mean the theme must be stated outright. In fact, heavy-handed thematic statements can feel preachy and artificial. Instead, the theme should emerge through events, choices, and consequences. What I mean is taking the theme you have written for editing and measuring the scenes against it.

Returning to the earlier example, *The Old Man and the Sea* never stops the narrative to lecture readers about perseverance. Instead, the theme emerges naturally as the fisherman continues to struggle despite exhaustion and loss.

When editing your own manuscript, look for places where the narrative reinforces—or contradicts—your thematic direction.

If your story is about loyalty, do the events test that loyalty? If your theme involves resilience, do the characters face situations that require endurance?

If a scene contradicts the theme, ask why—is it setting up the character for a fall? Showing a counterexample (in order to reinforce the theme later)? Both of these can work. The real danger is when a scene doesn't have anything to do with the theme, either in setup or support.

The more consistently the story supports the theme, the more unified the manuscript will feel.

Here's an example from my own (as of 2026 unpublished) work, *Art in the Attic*. The theme is that parents can't always protect their kids. Nate is a widowed father of 20-year-old Aurora and is seeing her in her first lead role when he bumps into an old friend, Angie. They watched the play together.

This is the first draft:

"Zylle would have been so proud," Angie's voice came from behind, and he realized with a start that she'd been waiting for him. "You want to try to go backstage?"

He hesitated, then shook his head. "She was saying something about a break-down party after the last show. I'll just call her in the morning." He looked back at the stage, as if he could see her beyond the heavy closed curtains.

"Hard to let go, huh? C'mon, then, let's go celebrate and swap stories. There's a little hole-in-the-wall Italian place not far from here. Great food, and they stay open to all hours." Without waiting for his reply, she started off.

They picked up his duffle bag from the coat check—he'd come straight from the airport and changed in the bathroom. The tired clerk smiled gratefully as she handed them their things. "I was beginning to think you'd forgotten it," she said as she pocketed the tip and started closing up.

They went in silence to her car then to the restaurant. It was a comfortable silence, though, the silence of old friends. At a stoplight, she turned to smile at him, and he found himself wondering at how he could feel so at ease with her after so long, but most of the time, he just thought about Aurora, how beautiful she was, how convincing she was, and how proud he'd felt watching her tonight.

When at last, they settled into the booth and given their drink orders to the waiter, Angie broke the silence. "You want to go first, or shall I? O.K. Lyle." It came out as a sigh. "I'm not sure what he was thinking when we got married. After we'd caught him and Zylle, he tried to convince me it wasn't what we thought, then he tried to tell me she'd been trying to seduce him and we came in as he was trying to get away. You know, I almost believed that? God, what an idiot I was. Then I went to the doctor for what I thought was an infection... Let's just say I had very real proof of his infidelities. I'll be damned if I was going to live with that. Sorry, Nathan, I know that you—"

"It's O.K. Go on."

"Maybe I just couldn't love like you. Anyway, I moved out; the divorce was amicable—Lyle really is sweet and loves me, in his own way. He pays good alimony, even though he doesn't have to. We were only married a year, but he really wants me to write seriously. His checks plus what I'm making in royalties and advances has kept me pretty comfortable."

It's not bad. There's some tension, a hint of romantic interest, and this is information we need later. However, as-is, it didn't really support the theme and in fact, moved the focus away from father/daughter to Nate/Angie.

Here's how it is in the current version I'm shopping around:

"Zylle would have been so proud," Angie's voice came from behind, and he realized with a start that she'd been waiting for him. "You want to try to go backstage?"

He hesitated, then shook his head. "She was saying something about a break-down party after the last show. I'll just call her in the morning." He looked back at the stage, as if he could see her beyond the heavy closed curtains.

"Hard to let go, huh? C'mon, then, let's go celebrate and swap stories. There's a little hole-in-the-wall Italian place not far from here. Great food, and they stay open all hours." Without waiting for his reply, she started off.

Bemused, he followed.

They paused in front of the poster for a selfie, then hailed a taxi and rode in silence to the restaurant. It was a comfortable silence, the silence of old friends.

Nathan kept looking at the playbill and the strip of paper announcing his little girl in the lead role. She'd been so good!

"She'd have killed him," he suddenly said aloud. He saw the taxi driver give him a look in the mirror and quickly added, "In the play, I mean. Aurora always thought vampire romances were stupid."

"Aurora, maybe," Angie countered, "but what about Marlena? That was a pretty intense last scene."

Nathan shuddered. "Some things a father should not see."

Angie laughed. "I thought you were going to leap off the balcony and bound over the seats to tear Lucien off her."

He had seen red for a moment, there. His hands actually ached a bit from gripping the chair. He dug his right thumb into his left palm. "I think I hate that Victor guy."

She took his hand and started to massage it, dragging her knuckles in circles over his palm, stretching his fingers back gently to release the tension. She had a firm, confident touch, and he found he liked it very much.

"Why do I think that if she becomes an actress, there will be a lot of leading men you hate?" she teased. She threaded her fingers through his, squeezed, and pulled.

"Father's prerogative. Where did you learn that?" he asked, indicating the massage with a drop of his eyes.

"I'm a writer, aren't I? Hey! We're there."

In the rewrite, I don't just mention that he's thinking about Aurora. He does so, real-time, and it's a mix of pride and protectiveness.

The dinner scene doesn't happen until Chapter Two, and even then, the focus comes back to Aurora when he runs into someone from his past he considers a threat to his daughter, overreacts, almost reaches for a drink (he's a recovering alcoholic), and resists because he has to think of his daughter.

Angie's divorce after catching Lyle and Nate's wife together is important, but doesn't come until much later, and even then, it gives an opening for Nate to wonder if he and Aurora would have been happier (and safer) if he'd left his wife for Angie.

The Nonfiction Equivalent: Thesis and Throughline

Nonfiction follows the same principle, although the terminology changes slightly.

Instead of plot and theme, nonfiction usually revolves around a central thesis and a logical throughline.

The thesis is the main claim or insight you want to convey. The throughline is the structure that guides readers through your reasoning.

When editing nonfiction, the key question becomes: Does every section advance the main idea?

During my decades writing for newspapers and magazines, I learned that conciseness is king. I still remember when I'd turned in a 1500-word story to *Fit Parent Magazine*, and discovered my editor trimmed it to 500! And it was great! When it comes to print, column space is limited. (I got paid for the full 1500, BTW.)

Electronic format has somehow only made us more impatient as readers. We want clear headings, sound bites, TL: DR (Too Long: Didn't Read) summaries.

Writing for AEO (Answer Engine Optimization) is the new skill for online writers, and it depends even more heavily on clarity of thesis and throughput because AI assistants, voice search, and featured-answer systems look for content that delivers a clear, concise answer to a question. That means the more strongly you support your thesis, the more likely you'll end up discovered and used by those engines.

The same discipline applies to longer nonfiction works.

Suppose you are writing an article about improving customer service in small businesses. You might include an example from a restaurant owner who changed her hiring practices and dramatically improved customer satisfaction. That anecdote supports the thesis.

If you wander into three paragraphs about the history of call centers because it's mildly interesting, the argument begins to lose focus.

The content may be good. It might even tangentially apply to the article, but it does not support the thesis.

Editing nonfiction therefore involves the same ruthless question fiction writers must ask: Does this section serve the central purpose of the work?

If the answer is no, it either needs to be rewritten or removed.

Complexity Is Not the Enemy

None of this means your manuscript must become simple or stripped down. Many excellent books contain multiple subplots, layered themes, or complex arguments.

The key is that those elements still support the central idea.

A fantasy novel might explore political intrigue, personal relationships, and historical mysteries, but those elements should eventually connect back to the central conflict. Likewise, a nonfiction book might include case studies, interviews, and historical background, but those components must reinforce the thesis rather than distract from it.

Editing for content is therefore less about cutting complexity and more about maintaining direction.

Your manuscript can take the scenic route, but it should still be traveling toward the same destination.

A Practical First Pass

When you begin the content edit, resist the urge to fix sentences immediately. Focus instead on the larger structure.

Ask questions such as:

- What is the central story or argument?
- Where does the narrative truly begin?
- Which scenes or sections move the manuscript forward?
- Which ones merely circle around the edges?
- Do you have the details in the right place to support the theme or are they more useful elsewhere?

You may discover that the manuscript already contains everything it needs. The problem is simply that some pieces are in the wrong place.

Or you may discover that certain beloved sections must be removed entirely.

Neither outcome means the writing was wasted. Those scenes helped you understand the story during drafting. Their job is finished—for now. You may be able to use them elsewhere.

The final manuscript only needs the parts that support the whole.

What to do With the Trimmings

Words are never wasted, nor is research. If you take something out of your novel or article, there are other ways to make use of it:

- **Promotional materials:** Create a short story or lead gen article around the extra material to draw interest to the book.
- **Behind-the-scenes looks:** Readers often want to know more about their favorite characters, so cut scenes make good extras.
- **Before-and-after:** Like in this book! Or use it in an article about your writing process or in an interview about writing.
- **Your next novel:** If a subplot didn't fit but you love it, can you play out the same events, motivations, etc. with other characters?

Looking Ahead

Once the content is solid—once every scene or section clearly supports the purpose of the book—we can begin looking at the sentences themselves. Some will already work beautifully. Others will need sharpening so the language matches the strength of the ideas.

That process is what we'll tackle next.

Content edits can be grueling—or they can be exciting. Sometimes both. I find I always learn new things about my characters—and often have even greater highs and lows for them in the rewrite. (In *Art in the Attic*, for example, I had not planned for the confrontation in the restaurant, but the rewrite set up the perfect villain for the story!)

Let's dig deeper into content by looking at how it's organized: story structure.

Reflection Questions

- ➢ Why is it helpful to put a manuscript aside before beginning the editing process? What kinds of mistakes are easier to see after gaining some distance?
- ➢ In your own words, what is the difference between plot and theme in fiction?
- ➢ Why can a subplot that is well written still weaken the overall story?
- ➢ What does the term "literary throat clearing" mean, and why does it often appear at the beginning of a manuscript?
- ➢ How does the concept of theme in fiction compare to thesis and throughline in nonfiction?
- ➢ Why does editing focus first on content and structure rather than sentences, grammar, or word choice?
- ➢ What advantages can come from removing material that doesn't support the main purpose of the book?

Exercises

Exercise 1: Finding the Heart of the Book

Write one sentence that explains the central idea of your manuscript. In fiction, focus on both the central conflict and the theme. In nonfiction, focus on the main thesis or claim.

This sentence will become your measuring stick during editing.

Exercise 2: The Sacred Subplot Test

Think of one scene, section, or subplot that you particularly enjoyed writing.

Ask yourself:

- Does it support the central idea you wrote in Exercise 1?
- Does it move the story or argument forward?
- If it disappeared, would the book lose something essential?

Mark it as core, supporting, or possibly expendable.

Exercise 3: Testing the Opening

Look at the first chapter or opening section of your manuscript. Ask:

- Where does something actually change for the character or argument?
- Does the story begin immediately, or does it take time warming up?

Place a note where the true beginning of the action or argument might occur.

Exercise 4: Theme and Thesis Check

Choose one scene (fiction) or one section (nonfiction).

Write one or two sentences explaining how it reinforces the theme (fiction) or how it supports the thesis and throughline (nonfiction)

If that explanation is difficult to write, the section may need revision.

Exercise 5: Saving the Good Parts

Identify a passage you suspect might not belong in the final manuscript.

Instead of deleting it, move it to a separate document titled "Cut Material."

Later, consider whether it could become:

- bonus material
- a blog post or article
- background for readers

- the seed of another story

Good writing is rarely wasted—it may simply belong somewhere else.

CHAPTER TWO

Structure and Turning Points

Once you know what your book is about, the next question becomes just as important:

Is the story—or argument—moving in the right direction?

A manuscript can have a strong theme, interesting characters, and beautifully written scenes, yet still feel slow, confusing, or oddly unsatisfying. When that happens, the problem often lies in structure. The pieces are there, but they are not arranged in a way that creates momentum.

Anne Lamott tells a great story about this in her writing book, *Bird by Bird*. (I highly recommend this book!) She talks about how upon getting a rejection from a publisher she really wanted to work with, she went in person to talk to the editor, and he told her that, as much as he loved the characters, the story didn't work. She took the manuscript back to her hotel and (after some tears and some drinks), she started thinking, "What if this happened here instead? And if I moved this here…" The reordered and rewritten book was published.

Structure provides the pattern of tension and release that keeps readers moving forward. Humans understand stories instinctively. We recognize when events escalate, when a turning point changes the direction of the story, and when a resolution finally answers the central conflict.

When those moments occur in the wrong place—or not at all—readers feel it, even if they cannot explain why.

Editing for structure helps you see whether your manuscript builds in a way that supports the story you are trying to tell.

The Shape of a Story

You have probably heard of the three-act structure. It appears in novels, plays, films, and even many nonfiction narratives. The terminology varies, but the basic pattern is remarkably consistent.

- **Act One (Setup):** The characters and situation are introduced, and the story's central problem appears.
- **Act Two (Confrontation):** The protagonist struggles with escalating obstacles and complications.
- **Act Three (Resolution):** The central conflict reaches its climax and the consequences unfold.

Each act contains a turning point that changes the direction of the story. These moments matter because they signal that something has fundamentally shifted. The character cannot simply return to life as it was before.

Think of *The Wizard of Oz*. Dorothy begins in Kansas, dreaming of somewhere over the rainbow. When the tornado transports her to Oz, the story's direction changes. Later, the discovery that the Wizard may not be able to help her creates another turning point, and the revelation of the Wizard's true nature leads to the final resolution.

Readers and viewers recognize these moments even if they have never heard the phrase "three-act structure." The pattern feels natural because it mirrors the way people process conflict and change.

During editing, the goal is not to force your story into a diagram but to check whether the narrative contains clear turning points that move the story forward.

There are Other Structures

The three-act structure is not the end-all of plotting. There are four- and even five-act structures. Korean dramas, for example, follow a four-act structure, Gi-Seung-Jeon-Gyeol.

- **Gi (Introduction/Setup):** Introduces the main elements of the story: characters, setting, general lives, etc.

- **Seung (Development):** Develops the main events, building on what's been introduced.
- **Jeon (Twist/Turn):** A new element is introduced, like a new perspective that changes how you see a character or a plot twist. This is usually the midpoint of the story.
- **Kyeol (Resolution/Conclusion):** Brings all the elements together for a final, often emotional, resolution.

If you'd like to explore other structures, Kevin J. Duncan's article looks at 11 different ones: https://kindlepreneur.com/story-structure/.

Genres Have Structures

In addition to the basic act structure, there are genre expectations. I once had a publisher that mapped out the structure for different types of novels—what event had to happen at what point in the book to make it fit. I wish she'd published them. They'd have been a great help to so many writers!

As it is, there is an excellent book that discusses this, *The Story Grid* by Sean Coyne. He discusses structure of stories in detail and walks you through the story structure for a thriller.

If you do a lot of reading in your genre, you'll start to get an intuitive feel for the genre structure and expectations, but there are plenty of resources online, including AI, that can tell you the general structure of a story.

For AI, I used the following prompt in ChatGPT and applied it to science fiction and to mystery. It provided tailored answers (although I have seen mysteries listed as 4-act structures instead as well.)

> You are an editorial assistant assigned to provide research for evaluating stories for content. Give me the industry-standard structure for (genre), including what elements must be included and at what page/percentage of the manuscript they should be introduced. Cite sources for the information.

Structures can also vary by age. For Middle Grade readers, for example, you need to introduce a problem that readers that age can relate to with the main character before the adventure begins.

When Structure Goes Wandering

While you can find a structure or beat map and evaluate your story against it, structural problems often show themselves intuitively. The story feels like it's wandering or you start anticipating a point or event that hasn't happened yet. Or you might notice that:

- The opening chapters take a long time to reach the real conflict.
- The middle of the book feels like a series of loosely connected episodes.
- The ending arrives too suddenly, resolving problems that were never fully developed.

Often this happens because the manuscript contains too many competing conflicts.

Writers love complications. I know I do—the more I can heap on my characters, the more gleeful I get! We introduce rivalries, romances, secrets, betrayals, and mysterious objects with great enthusiasm. New characters pop in and suddenly want the spotlight, and they're so adorable (or deliciously vile).

Remember what we said above about everything fitting theme? Same idea here: When too many storylines demand attention, the central conflict can lose focus.

The result is a book that feels as if it has five different plots, all competing for the spotlight.

During editing, look carefully at the major conflicts and ask which one truly drives the story. Supporting conflicts should reinforce or complicate the main one, not pull the reader away from it.

This does not mean secondary plots must disappear. They simply need to connect clearly to the main narrative.

The Problem of Too Many Acts

Another structural issue appears when the story seems to contain more than three (or four) acts.

This usually happens when a subplot becomes so large that it begins behaving like a second main story. Suddenly the manuscript has two separate narrative engines running at once.

You already saw an example of this in the previous chapter when I talked about the romance subplot involving Joshua in the *Madness of Kanaan* books. Those scenes were emotionally rich, but they started to dominate the middle of the novel. The story slowed because the reader's attention shifted away from the main conflict.

Once that subplot was trimmed, the book regained its forward motion.

Discovery, one of my earlier books, has also had the problem of too many characters with major issues to resolve. Looking back, I realize I could have removed some and made the book stronger. They all fed the central theme in this case, but it was more an issue of too much going on. (I still love the book, though. I think that it would work very well as a mini-series.)

Structure works best when every major thread ultimately feeds the same central narrative and doesn't overwhelm the reader.

The Order of Conflicts

Sometimes the problem is not the number of conflicts but their order.

Imagine a story that introduces the ultimate villain halfway through the book, then spends the final chapters dealing with a minor problem that suddenly appears near the end. Even if each conflict is interesting, the sequence weakens the overall momentum.

Readers expect the tension to rise as the story progresses.

Early conflicts prepare the ground. Later conflicts deepen the stakes. By the time the story reaches its climax, the reader should feel that everything has been leading to that moment.

The best books are a roller coaster—rises and falls in conflict, twists and turns, but always leading to the big climb-and-plunge at the end.

During editing, review the order of your major conflicts and ask whether the tension increases as the story moves forward.

Chekhov's Gun

Structure also involves recognizing which elements actually matter.

Anton Chekhov famously advised that if a rifle appears on the wall in the first act, it should fire by the third. Otherwise, it does not belong there. The principle has become known as Chekhov's Gun.

In practical terms, this means that important elements introduced early in the story should eventually play a role in the outcome.

Consider this opening to my story, *Jovian Heat:*

> They say that if man were meant to live on Jupiter, God would have given him thicker skin and hydrogen-processing gills. That same "they" also said if man were meant to fly, God would have given him wings. Of course, by 2867, we'd not only cracked our genetic code, but could stack the nucleotides like gods playing with toy blocks. We gave ourselves wings or fins and gills and skins to suit any environment we wanted, and to hell with what God wanted. In the end, we could alter our bodies to suit, but we were still human,

with the same noble desires to do what's right at war with the basest needs of our Fallen state. God wasn't letting us off so easy.

I sat at my desk with my feet propped up, staring out the window at the throng of life above and below me. The orange sky had taken on a reddish cast; the long-anticipated storm was coming at last, and while the meteorologists said it'd be a short one—only a couple of years—there were still whispers that Gravstead was going to be the next Red Spot. Looking at the number of movers on the flyways, I had to wonder if someone knew something I didn't. Not that I could afford to leave.

A sudden gust knocked a group of floating Jovians into traffic. Vehicles swerved. One bumped an unlucky floater, who fluttered off in the opposite direction, shaking his fist. I imagined a few obscenities in honor of our planet's namesake and his lovers were used.

I shook my head. Guppies.

These paragraphs do more than set up a sci-fi setting of genetically engineered humanoids on Jupiter. Genetic engineering (and playing God and losing), the storm coming, the Guppies being pushed by the wind are all important to the mystery that unfolds. Especially in a mystery, readers expect that.

If a mysterious object, secret letter, or suspicious character appears in the opening chapters and never becomes relevant again, readers feel a subtle sense of disappointment. They were prepared for significance that never arrived. It can alienate the reader.

In other genres, it also means remembering and really thinking about how you can use any element you introduced. Especially in science fiction or fantasy. My husband and I often yell at the TV characters who let some situation get out of hand when there's a piece of technology *right in the room* that can fix it!

The opposite problem can also occur. A crucial solution appearing suddenly near the end without any earlier setup is lazy writing. Readers experience that moment of discovery as a cheat rather than a relief.

Editing helps you track these narrative promises.

You ask two simple questions:

- Does this detail matter later?
- Does the ending grow naturally from the setup?

If the answer to either question is no, the story may need restructuring.

Mapping the Action

Structural editing sometimes requires stepping outside the manuscript and thinking like a choreographer.

Have you ever read a fight scene and thought, "That doesn't make sense"? Or maybe a character seems to have teleported somewhere else in the room—two characters are talking face to face then suddenly, one is hugging the other from behind?

When I was writing *Live and Let Fly*, I had the best scene. My dragon Vern had been taken prisoner by an evil overlord with a bunch of minions. However, my clever dragon was subtly taking them out one by one. Unfortunately, they kept getting replaced, and all the while the villain is monologuing. It's a funny scene, but at the end of reading it to my kids, my 10-year-old son, Alex, said, "Mom, you've got too many minions."

He was right.

I drew a quick diagram of the room and listed each minion by number. Then I tracked where each one moved during the fight.

The result was not only a clearer scene but also a more exciting one, because I could see exactly how the action unfolded.

Sometimes structure improves dramatically when you stop thinking only in sentences and start thinking in movement and space.

Structure in Nonfiction

Although nonfiction does not follow a traditional plot, it still relies heavily on structure.

Instead of rising action and climax, nonfiction typically builds through logical progression. Each section expands the argument, adds evidence, or clarifies an idea introduced earlier.

Editors expect this progression to be clear and efficient. Articles must guide readers step by step through the topic. If the argument jumps around or circles back repeatedly, the editor will notice immediately.

A well-structured nonfiction piece usually follows a recognizable pattern:

- Introduce the main idea.
- Provide supporting context.
- Develop the argument through examples or evidence.
- Address complications or alternative views.
- Draw a conclusion that reinforces the central claim.

Even in longer works such as books, the same principle applies. Each chapter builds on what came before.

Different types of nonfiction have their own structural expectations, too. The introduction for self-help books, for example, begins with the problem, then the author's credibility, then what the reader will gain and how the book is organized. Then it outlines the problem, provides the system framework, then its application, then addresses obstacles and ends with encouragement.

Interestingly, this can vary by culture, too. Greg Stahl in the Catholic Writers Guild noted that English speakers like to start with bold claims, then explain a little, then give proof. Meanwhile continental Europeans would expect a more gradual buildup of the problems before making any big claims. Otherwise, they feel you are twisting the evidence to support your claim.

Complexity Is Not the Enemy

Some writers worry that thinking about structure will make their work formulaic.

That can happen, but it's not necessarily a bad thing, Jim Butcher attributed the success of his Harry Dresden series to following the Hero's Journey structure. (In fact, he actually wrote the book on a challenge to prove that structure couldn't make a book great—was he glad to be proven wrong!) If you read his books back-to-back, you'll start seeing the formula. In fact, I discovered I could not binge them for that very reason. However, individually, the books are masterpieces of imagination.

Structure is not the enemy of creativity. Rather it gives it safe boundaries in which to play.

Structure provides a framework that allows complexity to flourish without becoming confusing.

A novel might contain political intrigue, family drama, and personal transformation all at once. A nonfiction book might combine research, interviews, and historical analysis. As long as these elements ultimately support the central purpose of the book, they enrich the narrative rather than dilute it.

Structure channels creativity. When each major element builds toward the same destination, the manuscript gains both depth and momentum. The reader is pulled along for the ride to an exciting and satisfying conclusion.

At this stage of editing, you are still working at the level of structure and movement. You are asking whether the events unfold in a way that builds tension and meaning.

Let's dig more deeply into things that can interfere with structure.

Reflection Questions

- ➢ Why do stories often follow a pattern similar to the three-act structure, even when the author does not consciously plan it that way?
- ➢ What role do turning points play in helping readers understand that the direction of the story has changed?
- ➢ Why can multiple conflicts sometimes weaken a narrative instead of strengthening it?
- ➢ How does the principle known as Chekhov's Gun help writers maintain narrative focus?
- ➢ Why might drawing a visual map of a scene help reveal structural problems that are difficult to see in the text alone?
- ➢ How does structure function differently in nonfiction compared with fiction?
- ➢ Why has strong organization become increasingly important for writers seeking traditional publication today?

Exercise

Choose a scene from your manuscript (fiction) or
a section from a nonfiction chapter.

1. Identify the purpose of that section.
   - **In fiction, ask:** What conflict or turning
     point occurs here?
   - **In nonfiction, ask:** What part of the
     argument does this section support?
2. Write a short note answering these
   questions:
   - What new information or change
     occurs in this section?
   - How does it move the story or
     argument forward?
   - Does it connect clearly to the central
     idea of the book?

Finally, look at the sections immediately
before and after it. Do they build naturally
toward and away from this moment?

This exercise helps reveal whether your
manuscript's structure forms a continuous
path—or whether some pieces may need to be
rearranged so the story progresses logically
toward its conclusion.

CHAPTER THREE

Flashbacks, Backstory, and the Temptation to Explain Everything

We've asked two big questions. First, what is the book about? Second, does the structure move the story or argument in a clear direction? Congratulations! That's the bulk of your content edit. Now comes the next challenge: deciding how much of the past the reader actually needs to see.

Writers accumulate background material the way hikers accumulate interesting rocks. During drafting, every piece can feel so important. You discover your characters' childhoods, the history of their relationships, the political background of the world, or the events that led to the current situation. None of that exploration is wasted. In fact, it often produces the insights that make the story feel real.

The problem comes when all that background tries to follow you into the final manuscript.

Flashbacks and backstory can enrich a story or article, but they can also slow the narrative to a crawl. During editing, one of your toughest jobs can be deciding which pieces of the past deserve to appear on the page and which should remain in your notes.

Let's explore that now.

When Flashbacks Earn Their Place

A flashback is a scene that steps outside the immediate timeline in order to show an earlier event. When used well, it can deepen the reader's understanding of a character or illuminate a moment that directly affects the current conflict.

Flashbacks can be exciting and highly emotional, sometimes even more than the current situation. Nonetheless, they must be used sparingly and only when they serve the plot or theme. They work best when the information they contain is both important and difficult to convey any other way.

A flashback is usually justified when it accomplishes at least one (but preferably more) of the following:

- It reveals a turning point in the character's life that shapes their current decisions.
- It shows an event that the reader must understand in order to grasp the present conflict.
- It dramatizes a moment that would lose power if merely summarized.

When those conditions are met, the flashback becomes part of the story's engine rather than an interruption.

When Flashbacks Become Detours

Problems arise when flashbacks appear simply because the information is interesting.

During drafting, writers often think, *The reader needs to know this*. That instinct is understandable but isn't always right. Readers rarely need as much background as the author does.

Flashbacks become troublesome when they do things like:

- interrupt the forward momentum of the story
- explain events that could be conveyed more efficiently through dialogue or implication
- are peripheral events that can be better exploited by showing how they affect the characters or story rather than sharing the event itself
- wander into material that does not affect the current narrative

One useful test is surprisingly simple: If the characters summarize the flashback afterward in the present timeline, the flashback probably wasn't necessary in the first place.

In other words, if the same information could have been delivered in two lines of dialogue, a three-page flashback may not be earning its keep.

The Momentum Problem

Stories move forward through tension. A character wants something, encounters obstacles, and makes decisions that carry consequences. Every time the narrative stops to revisit the past, that forward motion pauses or loops in on itself.

That pause is not automatically bad. Sometimes the story needs a moment of reflection. However, if flashbacks appear frequently or at moments when the reader expects action, the rhythm of the story begins to falter.

Think about the experience of reading a suspenseful scene. The ship is on Red Alert, the enemy is firing, the warp core is breaching— Is this really the time for Ensign McCray to have a flashback of how he wanted to quit the

Academy, but the kindly groundskeeper told him to believe in himself? Even if the moment brings a tear to the eye, the timing feels wrong. *Save the ship, Jeremy! Then have your touching memory that helps you grow as a person!*

During editing, look carefully at where flashbacks appear. Their placement often matters as much as their content.

The Author's Knowledge Problem

When you have spent months or years living with a story, you understand the motivations, histories, and emotional scars that shape the characters' decisions. The temptation is to share all of that knowledge with the reader.

But readers do not need the entire biography. Often, they need only the part that explains the current (or very soon to come) choice.

Readers enjoy discovering information gradually. When every piece of background appears immediately, the story can feel oddly flat because nothing remains to be uncovered.

When I wrote *Madness of Kanaan*, I had a lovely background scene that showed just how awful it was for Deryl to suddenly develop psychic powers at 13. But it didn't fit in the book because it didn't have much effect on his decisions living in a mental health institution at age 18. It was deep past and left deep scars but was not immediate. I kept the flashback and turned it into a short story for an anthology.

Part of editing is deciding which parts of the past should remain implied rather than fully dramatized.

When Flashbacks are TMI (Too Much Information)

Have you ever been cornered by that one guy who has to tell you his life story before answering whatever question you asked? Flashbacks can hit the reader the same way.

Readers come to a book with questions in mind: What's going to happen next? Will they get out of this mess? How will this character grow? When background information and flashbacks feed those questions, the reader is wrapped up in the story. However, too much background or too long a flashback can overwhelm the reader.

They can lose track of the plot—or worse, *you* can lose track of the plot. They can get confused about what the point of the book is. Is it just to relive the character's past or is he actually going to do something interesting now? Or they can lose interest because you're taking too long to answer the questions they want answered.

Background information is important. So is showing and not telling. However, not every piece of information needs to be shared in a full-blown experience.

As you look at flashbacks and long background explanations, ask yourself:

- How important is this information?
- How much time and attention does it need?
- How much attention is it pulling from the main event?
- Should the information be presented in a different way?

Flashbacks in Practice: *If Wishes Were Dragons*

Now that we've talked about how and why flashbacks work, let's look at some examples. I'm using my book, *If Wishes Were Dragons* because I know why I did or did not use a flashback and can give you some insight. However, when you read a novel and come across one, stop and ask yourself why you think it was included and whether or not it worked.

In this novel, Vern, a dragon who had all his dragon greatness (and much of his memory) taken in a battle with St. George, is sent back into his own past—a past he only remembers in spurts. He's the only dragon left and does not know why. He has only recently remembered he has a twin as the Faerie Queen mentions her in passing.

Flashback One:

This is the start of Chapter Five and is positioned as a kind of dream:

> I stood upon a mountain crag in the Himalayas, the air biting into my scales. I

was uncomfortable. I was furious. But I was not alone. All around the rocky mountainside were my kin, a bright patchwork of colors against the stark terrain. The sight of it would have filled me with joy if not for the reason for our gathering. The King and Queen of the Fairy Court had done the unthinkable. They had broken their covenant with each other and with God. Durrehkeh had called us to inflict punishment upon them.

"We should eat them." His voice bounced off the rock and echoed with power. He blew an arch of yellow fire that lit the dim sky. "Flame them. Destroy them all until the entire species is gone. God can begin again with a species more suited to obedience."

I saw his face, sharp and dark as slate, indignant and enraged on behalf of our Creator. Durrehkeh was the first of our kind, the eldestkin, and in those moments we all felt his power and authority. The others cowered before his fierce determination, but my twin Grislakeh and I argued him down. How long had it taken us? What had we said that finally brought him around? I heard myself arguing, felt the language flow from my mouth and body, but I could not make out what I was saying.

Nor could I bring up the face of my twin.

If Wishes Were Dragons by Karina Fabian (2020: Laser Cow Press), pgs. 71-72

The important facts here are:
- The fairies have Fallen.
- This is the start of the Fall of Dragons as well.
- Vern has a twin with whom he was close, and they often were on the side of the other creatures of Faerie.
- Vern cannot remember his twin.

I probably could have woven some of this information into the text, but I chose to use flashback for a few reasons:
- I wanted the reader to experience Vern's confusion and conflict.
- The flashback let me hide information from Vern (and avoid a lot of explaining or declarations of "I don't know" to the reader.) If this was in conversation, the reader would be left asking, "What did

they say?" and might feel cheated. Here, they experience the cheat with Vern. That makes it part of the story and not a missing part of the text.

- Vern will reunite with Durrehkeh and Grislakeh later, so this flashback gives a taste of how he feels about them without having to tell the reader how he feels.

Now contrast this with a time I chose not to use flashback but weave the information into the narrative.

No Flashback Needed

In this scene, Vern has just been fired from posing for photos at the Ren Fest because a woman complained.

"What do you mean, you lost your job?" Father Rich demanded. "It's only been a day!"

We were at a picnic table in the open area of Los Lagos's Renaissance Festival.

...

What should not have been hard on business was having a live, genuine Faerie dragon on the payroll. Not a fire-breathing dragon, of course. I couldn't breathe fire anymore. I hadn't breathed fire since my battle with St. George. However, it made things easier for the festival organizers since they didn't have to worry about extra insurance or fire codes. I'm telling you, though, after the morning I'd had, I was wishing God would return my flames to me.

"It wasn't my fault," I said again. "I don't even know how I insulted her. If I insulted her. She seemed to take offense at anything."

I paused to glare warningly at a lookie-loo who had stopped to gape at my magnificence and was lingering to eavesdrop on my conversation. A family took the pause as an invitation and dashed up requesting a photo. I posed, a fake smile on my face. Only an hour ago, I'd have made five bucks every time Daddy the Smartphone Photographer said, "Hang on. Let me try one more with this filter."

I was raking in some sweet treasure, too, until this human wearing a sword and a leather bikini that was supposed to be her "barbarian armor" approached me and said she wanted to have my half-dragon babies.

"All I did was try to tell her it was impossible. She's the one who decided it was because she was fat."

"Who's fat?" Owen, one of the members of my gaming group, asked as he took a spot at the bench.

…(Their other friends join them.)…

"Vern got fired," Father said, then rolled his eyes at my cry of protest. "It's not a sin, Vern, and they're going to find out, anyway."

"What?" Linda exclaimed. "How could you get fired from that job? All you had to do was stand around and be yourself."

I narrowed my eyes at my friends, daring them to take a swing at the slow ball she'd just pitched.

…

Owen passed me a burger. "That's tough. So, is it because you called some chick fat?"

"But I didn't! She said it. How would I know? I'm a dragon. I judge human weight by how long before I'm hungry again. Besides, in Faerie, plump women are more desirable."

"And you said that?" Owen asked.

"Something to that effect."

Father crossed his arms and leaned back. "So, you agreed she was fat."

...

"You see?" I said to my friends. "That's exactly how she took it. It went downhill from there."

If Wishes Were Dragons by Karina Fabian (2020: Laser Cow Press), pgs. 5-10

Now, I did have the scene with Vern and the irate woman. It's hilarious. Poor Vern! However, just like with my scrapped opening scene of *Discovery*, it brings in things that never come back in the book: the irate dragonwife-wannabe, Vern losing his job, even the Ren Fest.

It's an annoyance in a long line of annoyances, but not something that plagues his psyche like his lost memories of his dragonkin.

What the incident did do was provide a means for showing Vern's situation and his relationships with the characters who do follow him throughout the book. So rather than start with the scene or flashback into it, which would detract from those relationships, I used the important parts and pulled them into the opening scene:

- Vern can't breathe fire.
- The Mundane world still doesn't understand him (or the Faerie).
- Father doesn't let him get away with anything.
- His friends are not above teasing, but care about him enough to know when to hold back.
- Vern has a unique perspective on humans as a species: "I judge human weight by how long before I'm hungry again."

I could not have brought some of these up in the flashback, which meant the flashback would have gotten inserted into the deconstruction of the incident. Other things, like the weight joke, would have been caught up in the argument with the woman, and possibly even overshadowed by it.

When you have a past scene or background event, ask yourself whether it's more useful being fully experienced in reader real time or experienced as a past event to be discussed.

A TMI Example

It's not always flashbacks that can add too much information. Sometimes overburdening a scene with detail has the same effect.

Let's use a quote from my book *Gapman* for an example: Ron has just appeared as Gapman, a superhero. Later, he overhears Kitty, a reporter (and his coworker, of course) talking about Gapman and is thinking about it while he uses his superpowers to create gravel to fix the long driveway to his house:

> Could this be the start of a Lois Lane-Superman relationship?
>
> What she said about my eyes... I know she tried to pretend she was talking about my X-ray vision, but I knew she was lying. She had that crinkle along her nostrils she got when someone called her on her BS. Did she really see my eyes, or was it an eye/mask thing? If she looked into my eyes, would she realize it was me behind the mask?
>
> Boy, I'd love to stare deep into her eyes. She was so beautiful—and strong and fiery, and I hadn't had a date in...

I slammed my hands against the boulder. Break the rocks. I needed to break the rocks and think about the interview.

Gapman by Karina Fabian (2025: Laser Cow Press) pg. 74

Let's add some details:

Could this be the start of a Lois Lane-Superman relationship?

What she said about my eyes… I know she tried to pretend she was talking about my X-ray vision. I mean, she even said, "And he's superhumanly strong and that accent and those eyes—" but I knew she was lying. Why else talk about the accent, too, if she wasn't into it? Shoot! The accent is fake. Will she think less of me?

I pounded the rock in frustration. It split cleanly into three pieces. I piled one boulder atop the other and swung my fist in a large circle, almost like swinging a hammer at the circus, where you try to hit the lever hard enough to ring a bell. I'd never been good at that game. Now, I didn't even need the hammer.

Crunch-crunch-crunch goes the gravel. I wanted to get as many potholes filled with gravel as I could before nightfall. I was ruining so many gloves. Still, cheaper than paying someone.

No, Kitty was thinking about my eyes-eyes, even if she said otherwise. She'd had that crinkle along her nostrils she got when someone called her on her BS. Did she really see my eyes, or was it an eye/mask thing? Mom did make a really good mask for me. It's a flattering shade of green.

I sighed. What did I expect? Mom sewed costumes for all her stripper friends. She always wanted to make them look good.

Still, if Kitty had looked into my eyes, would she realize it was me behind the mask?

Boy, I'd love to stare deep into Kitty's eyes. She was so beautiful—and strong and fiery, and I hadn't had a date in so long—not since Shiela and the next day, she'd told me she was a lesbian and changed her name to Tranzformerz. At least we were still friends. She was a good editor, and I got a lot of work from her.

Kitty wasn't gay, I knew that. And she was into me. Well, into Gapman. She never gave me the time of day romantically.

I slammed my hands against the boulder. Break the rocks. I needed to break the rocks and think about the interview.

At what point did you stop reading? (It's okay if you did. That was kind of what I was going for.) The section goes everywhere—Kitty, the road, his mom, even past romances. Now, the last lines about breaking rocks just sound like more work rather than a man trying not to think about how beautiful his unattainable crush is.

Everything in here is true to Ron's character, and individually, it's interesting. However, crammed together, it detracts from the scene. Some of these details are in other parts of the book, and some (like Sheila) are waiting for another book.

When writing a scene, use the details that support the purpose of the scene.

A Nonfiction Parallel

Nonfiction writers encounter a similar challenge, although the form is different.

Instead of flashbacks, nonfiction often relies on background explanation. When writing an article or chapter, it is tempting to include everything you learned during the research process. After all, if you spent three hours reading about the history of a subject, surely the reader should see that effort reflected somewhere.

Unfortunately, that impulse leads to digressions. Remember the analogy of the guy who has to tell you his life story? This is like the guy who has to tell you the town history and gossip when you asked for directions to the nearest gas station.

Background information must serve a specific purpose. If the historical context clarifies the current argument, it belongs in the piece. If it simply demonstrates that the writer did extensive research, it will probably be trimmed.

When I wrote for *Fit Small Business*, for example, I was assigned to write articles about payroll tax law for small businesses. It's a complicated topic, but the point of the article was to give a small business owner a clear understanding of what and how much they had to pay in social security, unemployment, etc. I could have added information about how tax laws had changed or compared different states, but that would have distracted from the issue: *How much do I have to pay the government?*

As a result, the only time I mentioned something was when it had a direct impact on that question. I could mention last year's tax law if it had changed for the new year because that told people who had done taxes before to expect a difference. I could mention another state's law if they had a cooperative agreement with a neighboring state because that might affect how they pay taxes for certain employees. In those cases, it helped support the answer.

I interview artists for *Everything Brevard*. These people have interesting lives, and some of them want to share everything! Sometimes, they share the most fascinating stories, but when it comes time to write, I have to ask myself, "Does this directly impact their art?" If not, the story or factoid stays in the notes.

The same discipline applies to longer nonfiction works. Background should illuminate the thesis, not compete with it.

Finding the Right Balance

So how do you decide what to keep?

A good rule is to evaluate each flashback or piece of background with the same question you asked in the previous chapters: Does it serve the central purpose of the book?

If the answer is yes, the material likely belongs somewhere in the manuscript. If the answer is uncertain, look at how it affects the pacing of the surrounding scenes.

Sometimes the solution is not to remove the information but to move it. A brief line of dialogue or a well-placed sentence of narration can convey the same idea without interrupting the action.

In other cases, the background works best when scattered in small pieces rather than presented as a single block of explanation.

The goal is not to eliminate the past. It is to keep the story moving in the present.

By now, you have examined your manuscript from several angles. You have clarified the central theme or thesis, checked the structure of the narrative, and considered how background information fits into the story's momentum.

The next step shifts our attention slightly. Instead of looking only at scenes and structure, we begin examining how tension rises and falls within the narrative itself.

In the following chapter, we will look at pacing—what I like to call the roller coaster of the story—and how to ensure that readers remain engaged from beginning to end.

Reflection Questions

- ➢ Why can too much background information weaken the forward momentum of a story or argument?
- ➢ What distinguishes a flashback that serves the plot or theme from one that simply provides interesting information?
- ➢ Why do writers sometimes feel compelled to include more background than readers actually need?
- ➢ How does the placement of a flashback affect the pacing of a scene?
- ➢ What similarities exist between flashbacks in fiction and background explanation in nonfiction writing?
- ➢ Why can gradually revealing information create a stronger reading experience than presenting it all at once?

Exercise

Choose a scene from your fiction manuscript that has a flashback or a section from a nonfiction chapter that contains background explanation.

Write a brief note answering these questions:

- What information about the past does this section reveal?
- Why does the reader need to know it at this moment?
- Could the same information be conveyed more briefly through dialogue, narration, or summary?

Finally, experiment with one revision. Either shorten the background explanation or move it to a different place in the chapter.

You may find that the surrounding scene becomes stronger simply because the story continues moving forward.

CHAPTER FOUR

The Roller Coaster: Pacing and Momentum

By now, you've looked at what your book is about and how it's structured. You've trimmed subplots that wandered too far, examined where the story truly begins, and decided how much of the past belongs on the page.

Now we turn to something that readers feel immediately, even if they can't name it: Does the story move?

Pacing is not about speed. It's about movement and variation, the rise and fall of tension that keeps readers engaged. Plots are like a roller coaster. The story should climb, drop, twist, and level out—but it should never feel like a long, flat track or a series of disconnected jolts.

When pacing works, readers keep turning pages without thinking about it. When it doesn't, they start checking how many pages are left in the chapter.

Not Everything Should Be Intense

One of the most common pacing problems comes from trying to make every scene exciting.

Writers can fall into the trap of thinking that when it comes to action and high stakes, more must be better. So the story becomes a constant stream of action, conflict, and high emotion. Ironically, that approach can make the book feel exhausting rather than engaging.

A roller coaster that only goes up is not thrilling. It's uncomfortable.

Just like a good roller coaster has moments of smooth going before the next big thrill, stories need that contrast of peace and pressure.

Moments of high tension are more effective when they're surrounded by quieter scenes that give readers time to breathe and to process what just happened. Those quieter scenes can deepen character, clarify stakes, build the subplot, or set up the next conflict.

By the same token, even the coziest of stories needs some highs and lows or else you cheat the reader of the ride. Even merry-go-rounds have the horses moving up and down.

The goal, then, is meaningful variation.

During editing, look at how your scenes are arranged. If every chapter ends with a dramatic twist, those twists begin to lose their impact. If every scene is reflective and slow, the story may feel like it never quite gets moving.

Variation builds momentum.

When the Middle Sags

If there is one place where pacing problems tend to gather, it's the middle of the book.

The beginning has energy because everything is new. The ending has energy because everything is coming to a head. The middle can drift if the story loses focus or repeats the same kind of conflict without escalation or variation.

This often happens when:

- The character faces similar obstacles over and over without meaningful change.
- The stakes remain static instead of increasing.
- Subplots take over without clearly connecting to the main narrative.

You saw earlier how a subplot can grow large enough to compete with the main story. In terms of pacing, that competition slows momentum because the reader's attention keeps shifting between different narrative threads.

The solution is not necessarily to remove the middle material but to ensure that it builds.

Each major scene should either raise the stakes, complicate the situation, or push the character toward a decision that matters.

Two things to note here: First off, we're talking about major scenes. There may be scenes within the major scene that slows things down and gives the characters and the reader time to breathe and process. Also, rising stakes do not always have to mean rising action or rising peril.

Scene Purpose and Momentum

Every scene or section has a job to do.

In fiction, a scene might:

- advance the plot
- reveal character
- increase tension
- set up a future event

In nonfiction, a section might:

- introduce a concept
- provide evidence
- clarify an idea
- move the argument forward

If a scene or section does none of these things, it often feels slow, no matter how well it is written.

This doesn't mean every scene must be dramatic, but every scene must *contribute*.

During editing, ask not only what happens in a scene but what changes or enhances because of it.

Letting the Story Breathe

While conciseness matters, pacing is not simply about cutting sections or amping the tension.

Some of the most effective moments in a story occur when the narrative slows down long enough to let the reader absorb what has happened.

In fiction, this might be a quiet scene after a major conflict, where the character reflects or makes a decision. In nonfiction, it might be a well-placed example that allows the reader to see an abstract idea in action.

A quiet scene can still move the story forward if it changes the reader's understanding of the character or situation.

In the following example, Rae Marie is a pilot in the asteroid belt hauling live turkeys and drunks in a ship that's literally falling apart *en-route*. But because it's Catholic SF, there's a priest aboard, and between chaos, he holds an impromptu Mass on the bridge.

Meanwhile, Father read St. Paul's exhortation to Ephesians. "I...urge you to live in a manner worthy of the call you have received, with all humility and gentleness, with patience."

She snorted, then winced, but Father went on undeterred.

Once upon a time, she'd understood gentleness and patience. Then, her uncle, who had raised her on his trading ship, died in an accident that destroyed their ship and their cargo. The insurance was enough to pay the damages and most of her medical bills, but when she left the hospital, she was alone, shipless, and broke. Sixteen was old enough in the 'Belt to be considered an adult, but not old enough to secure an apprenticeship with one of the big companies. She'd wandered, taking scut jobs and trying to save enough money to get her pilot's license, and ended up on Waylaid. But it seemed like every step forward was met with someone pushing her two back.

One of her fares—they'd now lost the privilege of being called "passengers"—was licking the camera.

Patience? She'd used up her lifetime supply, and gentleness had evaporated even faster. Now, if humility meant enduring humiliation—that she continued to do in spades.

Now, if I'd just gone through the Mass, it might have satisfied my Catholic readers, but it would not have advanced the character by showing her background and motivation (which play into the ending later).

The key is that these moments still serve the overall movement of the book.

They are pauses, not detours.

The Problem of Repetition

Another pacing issue appears when scenes begin to feel similar.

The character faces a problem, reacts in a familiar way, and ends the scene in roughly the same position as before. When this pattern repeats, the story feels stuck and that frustrates the reader.

You may recognize this in action-heavy scenes that blur together or in dialogue-heavy sections where conversations circle around the same point without resolution. Or you may simply notice how the character has the same problem chapter after chapter after chapter.

Sometimes, there may be a reason for this—for example, you're writing the redemption story of a gambler. If he only gambles once in the book or only battles the temptation once in the book, it's not much of a story. However, each time he gambles needs to be different, not just in situation but in what it means to him and the plot. So, for example, we start with him losing big, making him want to change his ways. Then he slips—but wins. He tries to stay "sober" but then a friend invites him. The next time, he loses his girlfriend. Then he's at a very low spot—financially, emotionally, temptation-wise—but this time, he walks away. Even if it were the same track with the same greyhounds, each one feels different because they bring in something new and they build tension.

One way to spot repetition is to summarize each scene in a single sentence: (Character) does (action) (consequence). If several summaries sound nearly identical, the scenes may need to be combined, cut, or revised to create more variation.

Tracking Movement

Just as you mapped the movement of characters in a physical space, you can also track the movement of tension.

Try listing your scenes or sections and noting their relative intensity:

- high tension
- moderate tension
- low tension

If you really want to get visual, map it onto a graph and check the rise and falls. If you are okay with using AI, you can put your story into AI and ask it to generate the map for you. Here's what it came up with for my story "Gone Fishing" in *Space Traipse: Hold My Beer 10* (Coming 2026: Laser Cow Press).

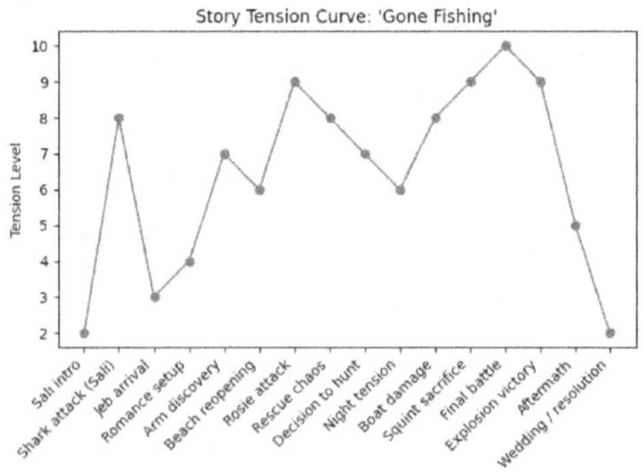

Source: ChatGPT

When you look at that list, patterns often emerge. You may see long stretches of similar intensity or abrupt shifts that feel unearned.

This kind of overview helps you see pacing as a pattern rather than a series of isolated moments.

While we're on the topic of tracking movement, be sure you note important steps. For example, in *Madness Unbound*, I had Deryl riding a unicorn BEFORE he put his clothes back on. Lady Godiva, he is not! I had to go back and make sure he was dressed.

Some actions can be assumed—if he opens a door, we assume he grabbed the knob—but when the omission is obvious (or potentially embarrassing), look for a way to fix it.

Pacing in Nonfiction

Nonfiction pacing works differently from fiction, but it follows the same underlying principle: readers need a sense of forward movement.

Instead of rising action and climax, nonfiction builds through progressive understanding. Each section should add something new—an insight, an example, a clarification—that moves the reader closer to grasping the central idea.

Pacing often comes down to conciseness. Space was limited, and readers expected information to be delivered efficiently. If a paragraph repeated a point or wandered into unnecessary detail, it disrupted the flow.

That expectation has only increased with online writing. Readers scan quickly. They look for clear headings, logical progression, and sections that deliver information without delay.

This is where editing becomes especially important for writers seeking traditional publication. Editors are not just evaluating ideas; they are evaluating readability. A manuscript that maintains clear momentum is far more likely to hold attention—and to be taken seriously.

At this point, your manuscript should have a clear purpose, a solid structure, and a sense of movement that carries the reader from beginning to end.

Now we shift our focus.

Up to this point, we have been working at the level of scenes and sections. In the next chapter, we move closer to the sentence itself and begin examining how language choices affect clarity, strength, and voice.

This is where the sharpening begins in earnest.

Reflection Questions

- ➤ Why does a story or article need variation in intensity rather than constant action or constant reflection?
- ➤ What are some signs that the middle of a book has lost momentum?
- ➤ Why can repetition of similar scenes or ideas make a manuscript feel slow?
- ➤ How does pacing in nonfiction differ from pacing in fiction, and what do they have in common?
- ➤ Why is conciseness important for maintaining momentum, especially in modern nonfiction writing?
- ➤ What role do quieter moments play in maintaining reader engagement?

Exercise

Choose a chapter (fiction) or section (nonfiction) from your manuscript.

1. Create a simple list of its scenes or subsections. For each one, write a short note describing:
   - its primary purpose (advancing plot, explaining a concept, etc.)
   - its relative intensity (high, moderate, or low)
2. Once you've completed the list, review the pattern.
   - Do you see long stretches of similar intensity?
   - Are there abrupt jumps that feel out of place?
   - Does each scene or section contribute something new?
3. Finally, choose one area where the pacing feels uneven and experiment with a small revision:
   - shorten a section
   - combine two similar scenes
   - adjust the placement of a quieter moment

The goal is not to perfect the chapter in one pass, but to begin seeing pacing as a pattern you can shape.

CHAPTER FIVE

Writing to Build Action

Up to this point, your work has been architectural. You've examined what your book is about, shaped its structure, managed backstory, and smoothed out pacing. Now we move closer to the sentence itself.

Most authors want to start here, because it feels more natural to fix sentences, polish paragraphs, or hunt down repeated words and adjust phrasing until it sounds right. If your first drafts are a hot mess of spelling and grammatical errors (looks in the mirror), then a certain amount of spelling and grammar check might be needed.

However, go lightly. Sentence work only matters once the structure underneath it is sound. Otherwise, you're polishing something that may not stay.

Now that your foundation is solid, however, sentence-level editing becomes one of the most satisfying parts of the process. You begin to see how small changes can sharpen meaning, clarify action, and strengthen voice. You've cut the gem; now you're going to polish it.

One of the most effective tools for doing that is understanding how your sentences handle action.

Who Is Doing the Work?

When you read a sentence, your brain looks for movement. Something is happening. Someone is doing something. Even in reflective or descriptive passages, there is still a sense of progression.

The question is whether your sentence presents that action clearly.

Here is a simple example:

- Cory chased the mugger.
- The mugger was chased by Cory.

Both sentences are correct. Both communicate the same basic idea. But the experience of reading them is different.

The first moves forward. You are in the action. The second one, however, places you outside, as an observer.

Readers may not feel that distance with just a single sentence, but it compounds over the course of a chapter. When too many sentences place the action at a distance, the writing begins to feel slower than it needs to be.

The Weight of Indirect Action

Passive constructions often rely on forms of "to be" paired with another verb:

- was chased
- were seen
- is being considered

This structure shifts attention away from the actor and toward the action itself. In some cases, that is exactly what you want. More often, it simply adds weight.

You can see this in sentences that layer extra phrasing onto a simple idea: *The decision was made by the committee to postpone the meeting.*

That sentence contains the necessary information, but it takes the long way around. A more direct version brings the action forward: *The committee postponed the meeting.*

The meaning is unchanged. The sentence is clearer.

The Difference Between Passive Voice and Compound Verbs

I remember early in my career being in a crit group where someone insisted on changing my verbs like "was running" because they were "passive." So annoying—and wrong.

Passive voice denotes a state of being. It's static in the moment. Just because a verb has some form of "to be" in front of it doesn't mean it's passive voice. Compound verbs in the form of *(to be) (verb)-ing* are progressive or continuous tense. They indicate ongoing action.

- She is running.
- They were fighting.
- I was tearing my hair out trying to explain that I wasn't writing passive voice.

So before you do a global attack on every form of "to be" in your manuscript, remember that progressive voice gets a pass!

When Passive Voice Serves the Sentence

All of this might sound like an argument for eliminating passive voice entirely. It is not.

Passive voice has its uses.

Sometimes the actor is unknown: *The door was left open.*

Sometimes the focus belongs on the object rather than the actor: *The treaty was signed after months of negotiation.*

In both cases, the passive construction directs attention where it belongs.

The key is control. Passive voice should be a choice, not a habit.

The Disappearing Action

Sometimes the problem is not strictly passive voice but a related issue: The action disappears behind unnecessary phrasing.

Consider: *She began to walk toward the door.*

The phrase "began to" creates a small delay between the subject and the action. In most cases, that delay adds nothing.

She walked toward the door. The revision removes the extra layer and lets the action stand on its own.

This pattern appears frequently in first drafts. Writers often build sentences that describe the beginning of an action rather than the action itself.

Sometimes, you need that start, of course: *She began to walk to the door, but her legs gave out from under her.* Other times, however, it's the literary equivalent of throat clearing.

You can do a global search with the Find function for words like "started to" or "began to" to uncover buried actions. Then you need to ask yourself—is the beginning the important piece or the action itself?

Words That Dilute Impact

Consider these two paragraphs: Which one gets you into the story faster?

> This might seem to be the story of my death—and my rebirth as something that felt newer, stronger, even greater, if you will. The story of how Ronnie Engleson appeared to burn in the fires of the phoenix and saw himself emerged from the ashes. At that moment, he'd become the hero he'd never known he could be.
>
> This is the true origin story of Gapman.

or

> This is the story of my death—and my rebirth as something newer, stronger. Greater. The story of how Ronnie Engleson was burned in the fires of the phoenix and emerged from the ashes as the hero he'd never known he could be.
>
> This is the origin story of Gapman.

Most people will go with the second version. The first version is wordier, but the problem lies in the nature of the words:

- might seem to
- if you will
- felt
- appeared to
- saw himself

These constructions, called "filtering words" or "perception verbs," often weaken the sentence by introducing uncertainty or distance where none is needed. They don't trust the action to carry the meaning, but bury it in prevarication.

Other words are fillers or "glue" words. They add bulk to a sentence without enhancing meaning:

- even
- at that moment
- truly

The words sometimes heighten drama, but more often than not, they are simply more verbiage between the reader and the impact of the sentence.

That's not to say that you should eliminate all of these instances—only that you need to be sure that there's a reason. For example, if someone is uncertain—say, watching a magic trick or seeing something while concussed—then "appeared to" may make perfect sense. If someone is being emphatic, then "truly" may have a place.

As you see these, try the sentence without it. Which way sounds better? Which one lets you (and thus your reader) keep diving into the story? Does removing the phrase bring clarity or cause confusion or distance?

Rhythm and Pace

Active and passive constructions affect rhythm of a sentence or paragraph. Active sentences tend to be shorter and more direct. Passive sentences often stretch slightly longer.

They also affect pace. Active sentences move quicker. They engage the present, feel more tactile, express in-the-moment. Passive voice is slower, seems gentler, has a sense of having more time. Used intentionally, that difference can help you vary the pace of your prose.

A sequence of short, active sentences can create urgency. A longer, more layered sentence can slow the reader down at the right moment. Just like plotting scenes can create a roller-coaster effect, sentence variation can keep a reader rolling through a page. More on that later. For now, the general rule of thumb is active voice increases tension and pace; passive voice calms and slows it down.

Nonfiction: Clarity and Authority

In nonfiction, these choices carry additional weight.

Readers expect clarity. They also expect the writer to sound confident in the material. Passive constructions can make writing feel indirect or worse, evasive, especially when responsibility is unclear.

Compare:

- Mistakes were made in the reporting process.

- We made mistakes in the reporting process.

The second sentence is more direct and more accountable.

That kind of clarity matters in journalism, business writing, and technical communication. It also matters in books intended for publication. Editors are quick to notice when sentences obscure responsibility or rely on vague phrasing.

At the same time, nonfiction sometimes benefits from passive constructions, particularly in technical descriptions: *The solution was heated to 100 degrees.*

Here, the focus is on the process, not the person performing it.

Just like in fiction, the goal is not to remove all instances of passive voice or slowdown words but rather to make deliberate choices not only for readability but clarity of understanding.

Patterns and Awareness

Every writer develops habits.

You may rely on certain constructions, repeat specific words, or default to a particular rhythm. These habits are not inherently problems. They become problems when they limit clarity or variety.

As you edit, begin to notice your patterns.

- Do you often write "began to"?
- Do you rely heavily on "was" constructions?
- Do certain filler words appear more often than you expect?

Recognizing these tendencies allows you to address them systematically rather than sentence by sentence.

Later, when we introduce more structured editing passes, you will have tools for identifying these patterns quickly. For now, awareness is enough.

Editing for a Professional Standard

Sentence-level clarity is one of the first things an editor notices.

In today's publishing environment, where editors are working with tighter schedules and larger submission pools, manuscripts that require extensive line editing face a disadvantage. Clean, direct sentences signal that the writer has already done the work.

This does not mean flattening your voice or simplifying your style. It means ensuring that your sentences communicate efficiently and support the tone you intend.

A distinctive voice becomes more noticeable when the underlying structure is clear.

Active and passive voice are only part of sentence-level editing. They help you clarify action and remove unnecessary weight, but they do not address everything.

In the next chapter, we will look at rhythm, flow, and word choice—how sentences work together to create a sense of movement and how careful editing can refine that movement without losing the character of your voice.

Reflection Questions

> ➢ Why is it important to identify the central action in a sentence, and how does that connect to the larger idea of supporting plot or thesis?

> ➢ What similarities exist between removing unnecessary scenes (as discussed earlier) and removing unnecessary words or phrases at the sentence level?

> ➢ Why can indirect phrasing weaken clarity in both fiction and nonfiction?

> ➢ How does sentence structure influence pacing and momentum within a scene or section?

> ➢ In what ways does sentence clarity contribute to a manuscript being taken seriously in traditional publishing?

> ➢ How does recognizing patterns in your writing connect to the idea of gaining distance during the editing process?

Exercise

Select a paragraph from your manuscript.

1. Identify:

- sentences where the action feels indirect
- phrases such as began to, seemed to, just, or suddenly
- any constructions where the actor is unclear

2. Rewrite the paragraph with the goal of:

- bringing the subject closer to the action
- removing unnecessary words
- clarifying who is doing what

3. Compare the original and revised versions. Ask yourself:

- Does the revised paragraph move more clearly?
- Does it better support the purpose of the scene or section?

You are not aiming to eliminate every passive construction. You are learning to recognize when a sentence carries its weight—and when it needs sharpening.

CHAPTER SIX

Adverbs, Rhythm, and Flow

In the last chapter, we looked at how sentences carry action. Who is doing the work? Is the sentence direct, or does it place distance between the reader and what's happening?

Now we turn to something a little less obvious but just as important: How does the sentence sound as it moves?

After all, even when your sentences are clear, they can still feel off. They may drag, repeat themselves, or fall into a pattern that makes the writing feel flat. This is where rhythm and flow come in—and where certain small words, especially adverbs, can ~~quietly~~ weaken your prose.

What is an Adverb?

If you know what an adverb is, just skip to the next section. But for those that don't: An adverb is a word that describes the verb or an adjective. (An adjective describes a noun.) Here are some examples, with the adverbs in bold:

- She ran **quickly**.
- He was **really** sorry.
- It was **just** there!
- He's **very** cute.
- She **always** says that.

Most adverbs end in -ly, but not all of them.

The Trouble with Adverbs

What's the problem with adverbs? Often, they exist only to shore up a weak verb or common adjective.

- She **dashed**.

- He was **mortified**.
- It **disappeared!**
- He's **gorgeous**.

Sometimes, though, they have a place. (I could not think of a better way to say, "She always says that," for example.) Also, some adverbs are weaker than others.

- Be **very** careful.
- Take **extreme** caution.

This is not a call to eliminate every adverb. It is a reminder to make sure each one earns its place.

When Adverbs Weaken the Sentence

The other thing is that they can be insidious. In my own editing, I've discovered that I have favorite adverbs. Once I start looking for them, I find them everywhere! Two of the most persistent are *just* and *suddenly*.

They slip into sentences without much effort:

- She just turned the corner.
- Suddenly, the lights went out.

At first glance, they don't seem harmful. They flowed naturally out of my brain, after all. But when you begin to examine them, you notice something interesting: Most of the time, they don't add anything.

- She turned the corner.
- The lights went out.

The action already carries the meaning. The adverb becomes extra weight.

If you notice that you have "favorites," then using Find can help you analyze and eliminate them quickly.

When Adverbs Do Their Job

Adverbs are not the enemy.

Sometimes they provide nuance that a single verb cannot capture. They can shape tone, clarify intention, or create rhythm within a sentence.

For example: *He spoke quietly.*

Replacing quietly with a stronger verb is not always straightforward. Words like whispered or murmured may not match the exact tone you want. In that case, the adverb may be the right choice.

Here's a real-world example where I kept the words "just" and "suddenly." "Just" gives that *almost there* feeling while "suddenly" announces Vern's surprise. Also, they fit Vern's conversational voice. (Emphasis added):

> A piece of his bandage hung loose behind him. Ha! I grabbed it in my teeth and pulled. Imhotep's momentum from his swing kept him moving forward, but my holding his band-age made him spin. Yes! I **just** needed enough to tie him to a pillar and—
>
> **Suddenly** a small, bandaged ball of fury launched itself at my nose. Hatsup!
>
> "Thanks for the Mummy-ries" by Karina Fabian (2025: Laser Cow Press), pg. 20

The key is to use adverbs intentionally rather than automatically.

The Rhythm of Sentences

Beyond individual word choices, sentences have rhythm.

If every sentence follows the same pattern—same length, same structure, same cadence—the writing begins to feel mechanical. Readers may not consciously notice the repetition, but they will feel it.

Variation creates movement.

Short sentences can deliver impact. Longer sentences can develop an idea or slow the pace slightly. Short paragraphs make readers read more quickly. Longer paragraphs cause them to slow down. A mix of both keeps the reader engaged.

There are two ways to check for this issue:

Look at your manuscript. Shrink your page until you can see the entire page on your screen. (In Word, that's the slider bar on the bottom right.) Do all the paragraphs look about the same length?

Here's an example from *Gapman*. Notice how the paragraphs vary from two to six lines.

¶

"You? You are Ronnie Engleson who writes for *Total Drama*?" they asked. "How? *Total Drama* is all about celebrating diversity on the screen, but you're so..."¶

Misty leaned her elbows on the counter. "What? Are you assuming Ronnie's heritage? Or maybe his gender?"¶

The person turned beet red and started sputtering apologies. "I, I loved your article on origin stories!" they concluded and hurried off before saying which one. I thought I saw their shoulders twitching.¶

I gaped at their retreating back. Should I go talk to them? But then one of the kids was walking out the door and it would have been awkward to pass him. "Are they okay?"¶

Owen chuckled. "Don't worry about it."¶

Misty added. "Pat comes in every couple of weeks and gives us or our customers a hard time about some misogynist comic or underrepresented character or whatever dumb thing an artist or writer said online. It was nice to use their own rhetoric against them for once."¶

She waved at the other two boys as they also left the shop.¶

Now, here's something I asked AI to write:

Chapter 1

It's Okay to Quit (Yes, Really)

Before we talk about perseverance, we need to talk about quitting.

Because here's the truth:

There is no shame in quitting.

Sometimes quitting is wisdom.

Sometimes quitting is growth.

Sometimes quitting is redirection.

Quitting might mean:

- Letting go of fiction and discovering you love nonfiction.
- Moving from novels to short stories.
- Realizing blogging is your lane.
- Walking away from traditional publishing.
- Leaving self-publishing.
- Releasing the dream of being a bestseller.

At one point, I had to quit my ambition of becoming a bestselling author.

And when I did?

I felt free.

Everything is a line or less. It reads choppy—it *looks* choppy!—but even more, it gives each sentence equal weight. The reader does not know what sentences support one another, so it's hard to know what the central point is. Also, it comes off as markety, almost like you'd expect in an infomercial.

Speaking of sound, that's the second way to check sentence variation. Read it aloud. Does it move naturally, or does it feel like a series of identical beats?

When sentences or paragraphs lack variation, they get hard to read—especially if the sentences and paragraphs are super-short. That seems counterintuitive, and yet, I've found it true. It's almost like the eye has a harder time tracking or the sentences cause it to speed up, and the brain gets ramped until it's taking in words without absorbing the meaning or emotional impact.

Avoiding the Pile-Up

Another common issue appears when sentences accumulate too many descriptive elements.

Adjectives, adverbs, and additional clauses can stack together until the sentence becomes difficult to follow.

For example: *She walked very quickly and nervously down the long, dark, narrow hallway.*

The sentence is trying to do too much at once. It tells the reader how she walks, how she feels, and what the hallway looks like—all in one line.

A revision might separate those elements:

"She hurried down the hallway. It was long, dark, and narrow, and the silence made her uneasy."

The information remains, but the sentence breathes.

You can go further and remove the passive voice and get into her head more: *She hurried down the hallway. The walls seemed to close in on her and the silence stifled.*

Notice I used "seemed to." I did so because the walls didn't actually close on her, but that was her perception.

Consistency of Imagery

As you refine sentences, you may also notice how imagery behaves across a paragraph or scene.

If a description begins with one type of imagery and then shifts abruptly to another, the effect can feel disjointed.

For example, mixing mechanical imagery with natural imagery in the same description can create confusion unless the contrast is intentional.

- **Confusing:** The viney cables entwined her arms. (Does that mean the cables look like vines? Are they green? Have leaves?)
- **Impactful:** The cables twisted, vinelike, entwining her arms. (Vinelike describes the motion of the cables. You can still imagine steel cables but with a creepy motion.)

Choose a metaphor and stay with it unless there's an intentional reason to mix them; then, be sure that the combo says what you intend. This gives prose a sense of harmony.

Flow Between Sentences

Flow is not only about individual sentences (or paragraphs) but also about how they connect.

Each sentence should feel like a natural continuation of the one before it. When transitions are abrupt or unclear, the reader must stop and reorient.

This does not mean adding extra transition words everywhere. Often, flow improves simply by arranging sentences in a logical order and ensuring that each one builds on what came before.

Head-hopping—abruptly changing the point of view from one character to another without any warning—often disrupts the flow of the prose. While authors most often do this when writing in the omniscient POV than when they stay with one or two characters and follow their POVs deeply, it needs to be handled well.

There is a poetry to moving from character to character. The best way to learn this, IMHO, is to read a lot of books in omniscient voice.

Omniscient POV with smooth head-hops is not as popular anymore, however. Usually, you should indicate a change of POV with a line break or at least a clear signal like naming the character before going into their view:

Harry laughed, finally feeling confident. Now, she'd understand the kind of man he was and how far he'd go to win her hand.

Leslie stared askance at him. *The man is a loon—completely mental. How could he think I'd find that attractive?*

Outside head-hopping (and in nonfiction), this lack of connection can come from trying to do too much in a sentence or paragraph. You may need to:

- slow down
- go deeper into a scene or explanation
- divide a sentence into several
- rearrange the order of the sentence or words

Here's the same scene with almost identical sentences. Notice how the order impacts your understanding:

I stood in the doorway, my wings spread wide and tail swinging. We were in an abandoned office in a Tokneo building, to prevent from escaping any of the hobgoblins we chased in there. Gapman was moving around the room, trying to reason with their leader and use his superhearing to locate each one.

"Please, Mister—"

"You assume gender?" came a deep, gruff voice from behind the file cabinet.

"Leesi," I called out to the hobgoblin's wife, "you got any doubts about his gender?"

True to his Mundane American upbringing, Gapman paused. "I, I apologize. I—"

Three of the others in the room also responded with catcalls. They had eight kids and another on the way. She responded with a giggle.

Now, I purposely mixed things up for this exercise. This was not my first draft. However, can you see the issues?

- Vern says he's in a doorway; then, he says they are in the office.
- Gapman is "trying to reason with the leader" and "locate each one." "Each one" in this sentence construction leads back to leader, which implies more than one leader.

- While Vern might have called out to Leesi while Gapman was stammering an apology, putting it in between the accusation and the apology gets confusing.
- By having the others make catcalls first then saying, "They have eight kids," it implies the others do, not Kenjo and Leesi (or that they are a community marriage).

This is the clean version:

I stood in the doorway of the abandoned office in a Tokneo building, my wings spread wide and tail swinging to prevent any of the hobgoblins we chased in there from escaping. Inside the office, Gapman was moving around the room, trying to use his superhearing to locate each one while he also tried to reason with their leader.

"Please, Mister—"

"You assume gender?" came a deep, gruff voice from behind the file cabinet.

True to his Mundane American upbringing, Gapman paused. "I, I apologize. I—"

"Leesi," I called out to the hobgoblin's wife, "you got any doubts about his gender?"

They had eight kids and another on the way. She responded with a giggle. Three of the others in the room also responded with catcalls.

Mensa, Magic, and Mayhem by Karina Fabian (2025: Laser Cow Press), pg. 2

One practical way to test flow is to read the paragraph aloud. If you stumble or feel the need to pause unexpectedly, the structure may need adjustment. Also ask yourself if the pronouns (including that, one, these...) refer to the nearest noun.

You can also follow the rule of focus. If you are drawing the reader's attention helter-skelter around the room or action, then consider reframing:

- Move from one direction to the next, such as clockwise, left-to-right, up-to-down, near-to-far.
- Move the focus inward or outward, such as body to face to eyes.

- Move perceptions deeper or more outward.
- Use a logical pattern of if-then, first-next. You don't have to label them, or you can start with the labels and revise to take them out.

Nonfiction: Clarity and Readability

In nonfiction, rhythm and flow affect readability just as much as clarity.

Online reading has changed how most readers absorb information. They move quickly, looking for clear, digestible information. Readers scan, skip, and return. Clean, well-paced sentences make that process easier while long, repetitive sentences or large paragraphs slow that process.

Adverbs can be particularly problematic in nonfiction when they soften statements unnecessarily:

- The results were somewhat surprisingly positive.
- The results were positive.

The second version is clearer and more confident.

At the same time, nonfiction benefits from well-placed variation. A sequence of short, direct sentences can present information efficiently, but occasional longer sentences help connect ideas and provide context.

Letting the Sentence Do Its Work

At this stage, editing becomes a matter of narrowing your attention.

You are not rewriting the entire manuscript. You are adjusting the language so that each sentence does what it needs to do—no more, no less.

Some sentences will become shorter. Others may expand slightly to clarify meaning. Many will simply lose a word or two that was never necessary.

The cumulative effect is significant.

The writing becomes clearer, the rhythm more natural, and the voice more distinct.

We have now addressed how sentences handle action and how they move.

In the next chapter, we will look more closely at dialogue—how characters speak, how dialogue carries information, and how to avoid common pitfalls that can weaken both clarity and character.

Reflection Questions

- ➤ Why do adverbs often appear in sentences where the verb is not doing enough work?
- ➤ What effect does sentence variation have on the reader's experience?
- ➤ Why can too many descriptive elements in a single sentence make writing harder to follow?
- ➤ How does rhythm contribute to the sense of movement in a passage?
- ➤ What similarities exist between pacing at the scene level and rhythm at the sentence level?
- ➤ Why is clarity especially important in nonfiction writing, and how do adverbs affect that clarity?

Exercise

Select a paragraph from your manuscript.

1. Identify:
    - adverbs
    - repeated sentence structures
    - sentences that feel crowded with description

2. Revise the paragraph by:
    - replacing weak adverb/verb or adverb/adjective combinations with stronger words where possible
    - varying sentence length and structure
    - breaking up sentences that carry too much information

3. Read both versions aloud.
    - Which version flows more naturally?
    - Which version is easier to follow?

The goal is not to remove every adverb or create perfect variation. It is to begin hearing how your sentences move—and how small adjustments can improve that movement.

CHAPTER SEVEN

Dialogue That Works

Dialogue is fun to write. Our characters come alive, share their thoughts, express their feelings. You can feed the reader information more naturally, and you get to play with slang and accent. However, good dialogue takes skill and understanding of where and how to use it.

When dialogue works, readers forget they are reading. They hear the characters. They follow the exchange. The scene moves forward naturally, carrying information, emotion, and tension all at once.

When it doesn't work, conversations feel forced. Characters sound alike or sound like caricatures instead of real people. Dialogue done badly can slow a story or even pull a reader out of the scene.

I'll be writing another book on creating great dialogue, but there are plenty of books on Amazon about the topic. For editing, we'll concentrate on making sure it's readable and that it does its job.

What Dialogue Is For

At its best, dialogue accomplishes several things at once.

It can:

- reveal character
- advance the plot
- convey necessary information
- create tension between characters

What it should not do is simply fill space.

A conversation that exists only because "people would talk here" often ends up repeating information the reader already knows or explaining things too directly.

In earlier chapters, we looked at how every scene must serve the central purpose of the book. The same principle applies here. Every line of dialogue should earn its place.

Along those lines, let me repeat—every *line* should earn its place. There's a saying that fiction needs to be more real than real life. That does not necessarily apply to dialogue. In real life, people seldom speak full, clear sentences. In addition to the "uhs" and "ums" and "So..." people start sentences then veer off like a drunk driver avoiding the median. Others make a point and never explain or trust body language to convey the point.

If you do too much of that in fiction, people get impatient (even more than they do when dealing with that face to face.)

> "Where were you? I mean, it's—what time is it now? Because I was sitting here, like, for over an hour, and I even... You have no consideration and now the pasta's cold."

> "I told you, didn't I? I mean, I texted—well, I thought I texted—maybe it didn't go through, but traffic was just ridiculous, like, there was this accident on I-95—"

"You always say that. It's always traffic or your boss or something, and I can smell the beer, but it's *never* the beer and was it a lager? 'Cause that makes all the difference. Mother warned me. She's coming over next week—don't be late again. I mean, do you even think about me sitting here waiting?"

"That's not it. What am I supposed to do, just leave work when things come up? That's not how jobs work."

"Get off the table, stupid cat! You don't respect my time, and I had a whole evening planned, and now it's just—ruined."

"Ruined? That's a little dramatic, don't you think? I'm here now, aren't I?"

"Yeah, now. After I've been sitting here getting totally more and more upset and wondering if I should just eat alone."

"I said I was sorry—well, uh, you know, I'm saying it now—and I just think you're making a bigger deal out of this than it needs to be."

This isn't necessarily bad, and it sounds pretty realistic—even the yelling at the cat. However, it's wordy and wanders. What point is being made here for the story? Is it that he's always late? Always making excuses? Or that he's blaming work and traffic and showing up smelling like alcohol?

Let's pick one and clean it up, keeping some of the idiosyncrasies of the character speech but drilling down to the point.

> "Where were you? The pasta's cold, and I've been worried sick."
>
> "You didn't get the text?"
>
> "What text?"
>
> "I thought I texted… So, traffic was just ridiculous, like, there was this accident on I-95—"
>
> "Please, stop! It's always traffic or your boss or something, but I can smell the beer on your breath."
>
> "It was a work thing! What am I supposed to do, just leave work because you set an early dinner? That's not how you get promoted."
>
> "Well, this isn't how you build a relationship! You don't respect my time,

and I had a whole evening planned, and now it's just—ruined."

"Ruined? That's a little dramatic, don't you think? I'm here now, aren't I?"

"Yeah, *now*. After I've been sitting here getting more and more upset and worried."

"I'm sorry. It was one drink, okay? Let's not make a bigger deal out of this than it needs to be."

As you tighten, beware of going too tight. Here's the same argument. I told ChatGPT to tighten it.

"Where were you?"

"Traffic. I tried to text."

"You're an hour late."

"I know. I'm sorry."

"This keeps happening."

"I don't do it on purpose."

"That doesn't make it better. I planned tonight."

"And I got stuck at work. What did you want me to do—walk out?"

"I wanted you to care that I was waiting."

"I am here now."

"That's not the point."

It's certainly snappier. Each line has a single, focused emotional beat, and the argument is straightforward. But we've lost the personality of the characters, and with that, anything that makes this argument interesting.

Also notice that the first six lines are less than six words long. Did your eyes want to scan fast? Mine did, and as a result, I lost a lot of the emotion. That's why varying sentence and paragraph length makes a big difference.

A final note: I took out the action and the he said/she said, etc. so we could concentrate on what the speakers said. However, good dialogue in books will include these things. Otherwise, it reads like a script, and you risk the reader losing track of who is saying what.

Speaking of, let's talk dialogue tags.

"Said" Is Not the Enemy

One of the most persistent myths about dialogue is that writers should avoid using said. I think it comes from our school years, where our English teachers encouraged us to be more creative with our dialogue tags.

In professional writing, however, especially in longer works, using a blatantly expressive tag—exclaimed, shouted, sighed, whispered—every time gets tiring for the reader and the writer.

In practice, said is nearly invisible. Readers process it without stopping. When you replace it with more dramatic alternatives, you often draw attention away from the dialogue itself.

Consider:

- "We need to leave now," she said.
- "We need to leave now," she exclaimed urgently.

The second version adds information, but it also adds weight. In many cases, the dialogue already conveys the urgency. Punctuation can sometimes take the place of heavier tags and still keep focus on what's said:

- "We need to leave *now*," she said.
- "We need to leave now!" she said.

The principle is simple: Said works because it does not get in the way.

That said (haha), don't use said exclusively. Just like with adverbs, there are times when a stronger, more creative dialogue tag works. When editing, evaluate the use of the tags. Sometimes, you can just sense that there are too many "shouted," "exclaimed," or "urged." They can start feeling like ants under the skin, or an excess of useless adrenalin. Meanwhile, if your character dialogue feels flat for the situation, then you might want to add a more expressive tag.

Action Beats vs. Dialogue Tags

A useful alternative to dialogue tags is the action beat.

For example, instead of writing *"I'm not going," he said stubbornly*, you can write *He crossed his arms. "I'm not going."*

Did you notice what word got removed? The action provides context and emotion without relying on an adverb. It also helps anchor the characters in the scene, which becomes especially important in longer exchanges.

It helps readers to see and even experience what's going on rather than being told what to imagine. In this example, the reader "sees" the character cross his arms and thinks, "He's being stubborn" or "He's standing fast." You don't have to tell them because you showed it.

However, just like creative dialogue tags, action beats can become cluttered if overused. Not every line of dialogue needs an accompanying action.

Here's an example of a mix:

Al'Beah's dark skin got a little blue, the genie equivalent of embarrassment. "Oh, no. I simply set events into motion. I'm the artist. I'm outside the work. I…" **(action tag)**

"No," I said, musing. "Father may have something here. Just imagine if you were a participant in your own art." I glanced meaningfully at my friends. **(said)**

"It'd be groundbreaking," Linda wheedled. "Visionary, even." **(creative dialogue tag)**

"Very meta," Owen added. **(creative (sort of) dialogue tag)**

"No," the genie said, his smoke tail shortening as he started to back into his lamp. "I couldn't, really." **(said)**

He wasn't going to fall for it. I gritted my teeth into a grin. "Oh, but you must. I wish it." **(action tag)**

"You—" Al'Beah called me the nastiest word in the genie language, but I grinned a real smile this time. **(action tag)**

If Wishes Were Dragons by Karina Fabian (2020: Laser Cow Press), pg. 138.

Variety keeps the prose and the dialogue interesting.

Don't Make Characters Cough Their Lines

Writers sometimes try to vary dialogue tags by attaching physical actions to speech in ways that do not quite make sense.

For example: "I don't believe you," she shrugged.

Shrugging is not a way of speaking. It is a separate action.

This may seem like a small issue, but it affects clarity. Dialogue tags should reflect speech. Actions should remain actions.

Keeping those functions separate helps the reader follow the scene without distraction.

There are exceptions, of course. What if the person is actually trying to cough their line? "I would never name names," Jake declared, then coughed, *"Kevin!"* In this case, Jake is combining Kevin's name in the force of a fake cough.

Sometimes, all you need to do is use a period instead of a comma: *"I don't believe you."* **She** *shrugged.* Other times, you may want to consider another verb.

Avoiding the Information Dump

Writers often use dialogue to deliver information, especially in speculative fiction or complex nonfiction narratives. It gives them the chance to educate the reader without a lecture because they can feed in the important information, ask questions, and put in a little character building at the same time. The challenge is to do this without making the conversation feel artificial.

If two characters already know the same information, they are unlikely to explain it to each other in detail. When they do, the dialogue can sound forced. For example, I read that *The Big Bang Theory* got a lot of pushback from academics and scientists because the characters (who were scientists at Caltech) sounded cliché. When Mayim Bialik (an actual neuroscientist) came to the show, she realized it was because the characters were explaining science facts to each other that they should have already known. She helped the writers change up the dialogue and the show became a hit lasting 12 seasons.

Dialogue that exists only to inform the reader has the same effect as the narrator giving too much background information too easily. When giving information, make sure that you respect what the recipient character already knows, and that it means something to the plot in that moment. Here's an example:

"Mr. Pepper, what was it that you told us last semester about the Spartans?"

"Eh? What about them?"

"When we were studying their military tactics. Wasn't there some code that the Spartans used to communicate with commanders in the field?"

"Yes," Mr. Pepper said, "a skytale. Not a very good cipher, I'm afraid, but it did the job at the time. You wrapped a long strip of leather around a staff, wrote your message down the length of the staff, then unwrapped the leather. A messenger carried the leather strip to its recipient, who had to have a staff of the same diameter in order to read it."

Cinch looked again at the carved letters, and at the flag wrapped around the flagpole. He turned and looked across the school yard. "Mr. Pepper," he asked, "how long has that flagpole been there?"

He pointed at the old cast iron flagpole in the middle of the school yard.

"Since long before my time. I would guess that it has to be original to the school. Why?"

Meteor Men by Scott Schad (2025: Raconteur Press) eBook version

This is a middle-grade reader, so there's more leeway on amount of exposition. Nonetheless, Mr. Pepper gives a concise explanation with only the most relevant facts. Cinch had enough memory of the Spartans using code to ask the right question and then to apply it to the problem he was trying to solve. (A secret code on the school wall.)

Other ways to reveal information are through arguments.

"What makes you think it's a conspiracy to attack you?"

"Because a bunch of robots and some humans are conspiring against me." Banneker draped a blue tarp over Winston. "Speaking of which, did you encounter any robots when you arrived?"

"Of course. This whole place is packed with robots."

"I mean, did any of them attack you?"

Ellicott shook his head. "No, they... well there was a tense moment with—"

"Tell me exactly what happened."

"Nothing happened, not really. Bishop went all 'override initiated' for a minute and I thought I was going to be attacked. And then Bishop let me walk by."

"That's bad." Banneker's brow furrowed, moving his hairline—something Ellicott rarely saw as Banneker usually had his hat on. "Very bad."

"Funny. I thought not being attacked was a *good* thing."

"It is," Banneker assured, impatiently waving a hand. "Of course, I'm glad you weren't attacked, dear cousin. Bully for you. But Bishop will have reported your arrival to whomever is behind this conspiracy."

Banneker Bones and the Cyborg Conspiracy by Rob Kent (2021: Rob Kent), eBook version

This is another middle-grade book, with two kids giving the information. Although Banneker is the smarter of the two, he still speaks like a precocious child. The two react to each other as cousins would. Banneker does not just come in with a declaration that the robots might be working for someone else and Elliot needs to be careful; instead, the information comes out in the back-and-forth.

Dialogue works best when it provides information on multiple levels: straight, plot-needed facts, insight into characters and relationships, and emotional impact.

As you look over the "info dumps" in your story, ask yourself:

- How much do I really need?
- Am I respecting the intelligence and knowledge of the character receiving the information?
- Does this sound conversational or lecturing? (Note: Use lectures sparingly.)
- Is the dialogue segment also imparting other information about the characters, theme, emotional stakes?

Distinct Voices

Characters should not all sound the same.

One of my favorite exercises I ever did was in a workshop by Devon Ellington, where she challenged us to write a scene with seven characters all talking—without any dialogue tags. We had to rely on their spoken words alone to differentiate them.

I'll be writing a book on dialogue later, but for the sake of editing, know that you can differentiate characters by their use of vocabulary, sentence structure, and tone. Accents also work, but you need to be careful not to make the written accent too hard to read or too cliché, and giving everyone a different accent gets complex and tiring for the reader as well.

As you go through the dialogue in your stories, ask yourself:

- Does one character speak in short, direct sentences?
- Does another use more formal language?
- Does someone avoid answering questions directly?
- What's the character's dominant sense? Some people say, "I see what you mean," while others might say "I feel you!" If you find two characters sound too much alike, changing their dominant sense and

finding the associated words can make a difference.

These patterns create unique voices that are easier to follow.

Dialogue and Pacing

Dialogue naturally speeds up a scene. It breaks up paragraphs and creates a sense of immediacy.

However, long stretches of dialogue without the addition of actions, scene setting, or interior thoughts get difficult to follow, especially if multiple characters are speaking. On the other hand, too many interruptions can slow the exchange to a crawl.

Let's go back to the argument scene. Can we take the sparse and dry dialogue ChatGPT generated and make it interesting with pacing?

Before:

"Where were you?"

"Traffic. I tried to text."

"You're an hour late."

"I know. I'm sorry."

"This keeps happening."

"I don't do it on purpose."

"That doesn't make it better. I planned tonight."

"And I got stuck at work. What did you want me to do—walk out?"

"I wanted you to care that I was waiting."

"I am here now."

"That's not the point."

Although I asked AI to create this example, authors sometimes write this way, not out of laziness but because they are in the scene themselves. They feel what the characters feel, see what they see—and because they have set up the situation, they believe the readers are in the scene with them. But you can't rely on that. You need to show the reader.

Sometimes, too, a writer might be writing something that impacts them personally, and so they skirt over the writing that would make the heavy impact because it's uncomfortable for them, too. If that's you, I have two thoughts:

One, we grow in the uncomfortable places. Two, writing can work to expose old wounds—and thus, help them heal. It may be hard to dig into a painful scene, even if it's a character and not you, but face it honestly, and you may find comfort at the end as well as put out some first-rate prose!

OK! Back to the example. Here's an After with tags and action to provide context:

Aliana ran to the door, hands outstretched, as Bruce entered, but stopped halfway. She crossed her arms instead. "Where were you?"

"Traffic. I tried to text." He sighed and dropped his keys into the dish by the door.

Traffic. Right. It's a 20-minute drive. "You're an hour late."

"I know. I'm sorry," he snapped.

"This keeps happening."

He rolled his eyes. "I don't do it on purpose."

"That doesn't make it better. I planned tonight." She pointed to the dining room table, set with dishes now cold and candles now burned halfway.

"And I got stuck at work," he replied with infuriating calm. "What did you want me to do—walk out?"

"I wanted you to care that I was waiting."

He shrugged. "I'm here now."

Why did he have to do this? Why did he always have to make it so I'm the unreasonable one? Tears filled her eyes. "That's not the point."

The first version reads faster, but loses the emotional appeal. Notice the paragraph lengths, too. Weren't they easier on the eyes?

As with pacing at the scene level, variation matters.

Short exchanges can create tension. Longer responses can develop ideas or reveal character. Use of action, interior thoughts, and dialogue tags add context and variation. Together, they shape how the scene impacts the reader.

Nonfiction: Dialogue and Voice

Nonfiction uses dialogue differently. You may not have a traditional back-and-forth so much as the strategic use of quotes, but the principles still apply.

In interviews, memoir, and narrative nonfiction, dialogue can bring immediacy and authenticity to the material. It allows readers to hear the voices of real people and see how conversations unfold.

At the same time, clarity remains essential. Quotations should be accurate, relevant, and integrated smoothly into the surrounding text. They should not repeat something said earlier, but provide more context, color, and information.

Bad:

> Pagliarini met artist Maxine Trainer at Trainer's studio, where she fell in love with a painting for its bright colors and theme of hope for the future. Maxine was so charmed by Pagliarini and her dreams that she gave the painting to her to adorn the walls of her future nonprofit.

"She started telling me about her dream to start a nonprofit and that she'd want to hang the painting in the office, and I loved the idea so much, I gave her the painting," Trainer said.

Pagliarini said that she was drawn to the painting's brightness and hope. "Her work reflects strength and possibility, not deficit. At a time when I was stepping into leadership, that perspective mattered deeply to me."

Better:

Pagliarini met artist Maxine Trainer at Trainer's studio, where she fell in love with a painting.

"She started telling me about her dream to start a nonprofit and that she'd want to hang the painting in the office, and I loved the idea so much, I gave her the painting," Trainer said.

Pagliarini said that she was drawn to the painting's brightness and hope. "Her work reflects strength and possibility, not deficit. At a time when I was stepping into leadership, that perspective mattered deeply to me."

"Cocoa Roundhouse Mural Shines With Hope for Families Facing Homelessness" by Karina Fabian, *Everything Brevard*, 3/1/2026

Whether in an article with limited word count or a longer book, quotations must earn their place just as much as any other element. A quote that repeats information or adds nothing new will often be cut. On the other hand, when a quote can take the place of an explanation by the narrator, it can add variety and a change of pace to keep the reader engaged.

Editing for Professional Clarity

When you edit dialogue, strive for clarity. Even if the characters are being deliberately confusing in their words, you should strive to make what they say easy to read and understandable.

Confusing exchanges, inconsistent voices, or overly elaborate tags can slow the reading experience and create unnecessary work for the reader.

This does not mean stripping personality from the characters. It means ensuring that the dialogue supports the story rather than competing with it.

At this point, you have worked through content, structure, pacing, and sentence-level clarity. Dialogue adds another layer, bringing characters and ideas directly onto the page.

In the next chapter, we will look at how all of these elements come together under a broader concept of beauty—how clarity, consistency, and purpose create writing that feels complete.

Reflection Questions

> ➤ What roles can dialogue play in a story or piece of nonfiction?
>
> ➤ When is "said" more effective than more elaborate dialogue tags?
>
> ➤ What problems arise when dialogue is used primarily to deliver information?
>
> ➤ How do action beats differ from dialogue tags, and what purpose do they serve?
>
> ➤ Why is it important for characters to have distinct voices?
>
> ➤ How does dialogue influence pacing within a scene or section?

Exercise

Select a dialogue-heavy scene (fiction) or a section with quotations (nonfiction).

1. Identify:
    - dialogue tags
    - action beats
    - lines that primarily deliver information
2. Revise the passage by:
    - simplifying dialogue tags where possible
    - replacing adverb-heavy tags with action beats
    - trimming or reworking lines that feel like information dumps
3. Read the revised version aloud.
    - Is it easier to follow?
    - Do the voices sound more distinct?
    - Does the scene move more naturally?

The goal is not to reduce dialogue but to ensure that it works as hard as the rest of your manuscript.

CHAPTER EIGHT

Beauty: Focus, Flow, and the Right Amount of Flowery

By this point, you have worked through structure, pacing, and sentence/paragraph-level clarity. You have trimmed what does not belong, strengthened what does, and made sure your sentences carry their weight.

Now we arrive at something that is harder to define but easy to recognize when it is missing.

Does the writing feel whole?

Not just correct. Not just clear. *Whole.*

This is the stage where editing moves beyond fixing problems and begins to shape the reading experience. Here, you make sure the parts of your manuscript start to work together instead of simply existing side by side.

Sometimes you hear people talk about beautiful prose. That can call up images of poetry or literary prose with deep and expressive metaphors. If you are poetic and lyrical, that's awesome!

However, even the most basic nonfiction article can have beauty when the writing feels consistent, intentional, and complete. That's the beauty we'll be striving for as we edit.

Clarity and Purple Prose

Before anything else, beauty depends on clarity.

If a sentence is confusing, no amount of stylistic polish will make it pretty. Readers cannot appreciate rhythm, imagery, or tone if they have to stop and untangle meaning.

We used to call this "purple prose" or "overwriting." Fun fact: The Bulwer-Lutton

Fiction contest is an annual award for the most intentionally bad, overly ornate writing. The entries are hilarious. https://www.bulwer-lytton.com. However, most end in a punch line. True purple prose takes itself very seriously.

Here's the prose that inspired the contest:

It was a dark and stormy night; the rain fell in torrents—except at occasional intervals, when it was checked by a violent gust of wind which swept up the streets (for it is in London that our scene lies), rattling along the housetops, and fiercely agitating the scanty flame of the lamps that struggled against the darkness.

Paul Clifford by Sir Edward Bulwer-Lytton (originally 1830, this edition, 1999: Kessinger Publishing), pg. 235

Here's a shorter example from my book, *Madness Unbound*:

Old: He was aware, too, of how hard Tasmae had hit him and how much his neck and throat ached.
New: His neck throbbed from Tasmae's choking and his head with it.

Here, the prose isn't flowery, so much as wordy. "Throbbed" tells us he was attacked. The details (hit and choke) don't need to be said.

This doesn't mean you can't be descriptive, even flowery, in your writing. Here's an example from *The Secret Life of Bees* by Sue Monk Kidd. It's one of the few literary books I've ever loved, simply because of the language:

> Finally, sometime close to midnight, when my eyelids had nearly given up the strain of staying open, a purring noise started over in the corner, low and vibrating, a sound you could almost mistake for a cat. Moments later, shadows moved like spatter paint along the walls, catching the light when they passed the window so I could see the outline of wings. The sound swelled in the dark till the entire room was pulsating, till the air itself became alive and matted with bees. They lapped around my body, making me the perfect center of a whirlwind cloud. I could not hear myself think for all the bee hum.

Secret Life of Bees by Sue Monk Kidd (2003: Penguin Books), pg. 4

What makes this flowery prose beautiful while Bulwer-Lytton's lumbers? Focus. Purpose. Flow. But above all, Clarity. There aren't asides to tell you something. The prose doesn't jump about in one long, confused sentence. Rather, Kidd's entire paragraph is dedicated to making you experience what Lily Owens experiences.

Clarity is not the absence of style. It is what allows style to be understood.

We've discussed a lot about clarity already when we talked about tightening sentences, clarifying action, and removing unnecessary words. All of these can help eliminate purple prose that does not work.

Now, you need to ask yourself: Does this sentence or paragraph serve the scene, or is it merely decorative? Have I tried too hard to be clever, lyrical, or amusing and lost the substance of the prose?

Lyrical vs. Purely Decorative Writing

Lyrical prose doesn't always take away form writing. In fact, the use of descriptive speech, similes, and metaphors can pull a reader into an experience in ways simple narration cannot. Consider the example above:

- *low and vibrating, a sound you could almost mistake for a cat:* It shows that Lily doesn't find the arrival of the bees threatening.

- *pulsating, till the air itself became alive and matted with bees*: Kidd doesn't tell you the bees are flying near. You feel it.

- *making me the perfect center of a whirlwind cloud*: "Perfect center"—it's a positive thing; she's not stung or molested, but protected. I imagine the motion, the swirling, like she's in the eye of the storm.

Sometimes, too, genre calls for a more lyrical language, especially literary and noir. (Look again at my noir SF mystery, *Jovian Heat*, which is heavy on style in the opening.)

They say that if man were meant to live on Jupiter, God would have given him thicker skin and hydrogen-processing gills. That same "they" also said if man were meant to fly, God would have given him wings. Of course, by 2867, we'd not only cracked our genetic code, but could stack the nucleotides like gods playing with toy blocks. We gave ourselves wings or fins and gills and skins to suit any environment we wanted, and to hell with what God wanted. In the end, we could alter our bodies to suit, but we were still human, with the same noble desires to do what's right at war with the basest needs of our Fallen state. God wasn't letting us off so easy.

Jovian Heat by Karina Fabian (2022: Laser Cow Press) pg. 1

As you go over your prose ask yourself:

- Is there a hidden metaphor or simile I can develop?
- Can I enhance the imagery?
- Am I meeting genre expectations for the prose?

Harmony Across the Page

Harmony means the elements of your writing work together. It shows up in several ways:

- consistent tone

- compatible imagery
- a sense that the language belongs to the same world as the story or argument

When harmony is missing, the writing can feel uneven. A serious moment may suddenly shift into humorous phrasing. A lyrical description may sit awkwardly next to blunt, functional language.

This does not mean everything must sound the same. Variation is important. But the variations should feel intentional rather than accidental. It also needs to fuel the mood.

For example, I open *Madness of Love* with a beautiful, flowing description of Sachiko's wedding kimono. I wanted to end with Sachiko wanting to destroy it. At first, I imagined this:

> The sheer kimono that lay over the dress didn't help. It was much too dainty, with the pastel flowers so sweetly and intricately stitched. It was made for mincing. Every flower, every shade, seemed to say, "Here is the gentle, submissive bride approaching her wedding with humility." To top it off, literally as well as figuratively, the white swath of the tsunokakushi headdress reminded her the good bride hides her independent nature.

Sachiko pointed her laser scalpel at it.

Sobo could have gotten me the dress I wanted. Instead she brought this.

I liked it, but my critique group said it was too abrupt. They didn't understand her violent reaction. So, I softened it to blend more with the tone of the first paragraph.

The sheer kimono that lay over the dress didn't help. It was much too dainty, with the pastel flowers so sweetly and intricately stitched. It was made for mincing. Every flower, every shade, seemed to say, "Here is the gentle, submissive bride approaching her wedding with humility." To top it off, literally as well as figuratively, the white swath of the tsunokakushi headdress reminded her the good bride hides her independent nature.

Sachiko pointed her laser scalpel at it and imagined tracing a path across the tsunokakushi, down the piping at the collar and along the obi-jime cord—a stripe of satin more decorative than useful that made a pale highlight around the waist. One flick with her finger and the ensemble would go up in smoke.

Sobo could have gotten me the dress I wanted, the one I asked for. Instead she brought this.

Madness of Love by Karina Fabian (2025: Laser Cow Press), pgs. 3-4

The best way to check for tone is in a clean read-through. Listen to how your voice changes, the rhythm of your speech. Where there's an abrupt change, ask yourself: Does it serve the story?

Choosing the Right Detail

The right details enhance the beauty of a prose, while the wrong ones create disunity and confusion.

Earlier, we touched on the idea that details should support the purpose of the scene. At the sentence level, that principle becomes more precise. The detail should reinforce tone, character, or theme.

So how do you choose the right details? In fiction, the character usually decides because everything depends on how they experience the world. When a character focuses on a specific object or action, that choice reveals something about their priorities, their emotional state, or their relationship to the situation.

Here's a bit from an unpublished work of mine, *Otherworld*, in which a priest enters a virtual reality world to try to remind people that true worship—true life—must be done in the real world.

> I arrived inside my little chapel on the main drag of the Station. Donations of virtual credit had brought about its creation; it was tiny, but beautiful.
>
> And real. Amazingly real. I could see dust dancing in the colored light streaming through stained-glass windows. I moved, and heard the swish of my cassock and the echo of my footsteps on the marble. I stepped with heel, then toe, marveling at the different tones. I caressed the smooth back of the oak pews. I even brought a missalette to my nose and breathed in the scent of the paper. Suddenly, I laughed and spun, dancing in my little church like David in the sanctuary. Like David, I felt full of joy and so very, very alive!

Then my ecstatic steps brought me before the form of our Savior crucified, and I fell to my knees, ashamed. I'd had my first taste of the temptations of Otherworld.

See how every detail, despite being for the different senses, is focused on the purpose of showing how real Otherworld feels to Father?

Choosing the right details also helps build a mood. Consider this paragraph from *The Night Circus* by Erin Morgenstern:

> The towering tents are striped in white and black, no golds and crimsons to be seen. No color at all, save for the neighboring trees and the grass of surrounding fields. Black-and-white stripes on a grey sky; countless tents of varying shapes and sizes, with an elaborate wrought-iron fence encasing them in a colorless world...
>
> *The Night Circus* by Erin Morgenstern (2012: Anchor Books), pg. 1

See how she took one detail—the monochromatic color scheme—and leveraged it to build the mystery?

Too many details can blur focus. The reader is given so much information that nothing stands out. A truly beautiful sentence or paragraph has a laser focus that extracts a grander meaning.

Consistency of Voice

Your voice is not something you add during editing. It's already there, waiting to be polished in your editing. That happens as you cut out the clutter and lean into what makes your story unique.

When sentences are cluttered or inconsistent, voice gets buried. As you refine, the natural patterns of your writing become more visible.

Consistency does not mean sameness. It means that the reader can recognize the voice as belonging to the same speaker throughout the work.

In fiction, this applies both to the narrative voice and to the way characters express themselves. In nonfiction, it applies to the author's presence on the page.

As you are editing, think about the parts that you absolutely love. Try to go beyond the emotional impression. What are you most proud of? What tone, detail, expression are you using that hits home?

Hold onto that information so that when you run across a part that feels drier, you can ask yourself how you can apply those elements.

For example, my favorite scenes in my *Space Traipse* stories aren't just funny but are where I found a great twist on the character or cliché. So when I go back over a story, I ask myself if I'm missing a cliché or an aspect of the character that needs twisting.

Flow Across Paragraphs

Beautiful prose has flow, that means the sentences move easily to the next, the paragraphs follow, and the chapter ends in a way that makes the reader quickly turn to the next page.

There are lots of ways to ensure this:

- The ideas in each paragraph can build to a crescendo.
- The paragraph before asks a question that the next one answers or acknowledges it. (Although generally not in the literal sense.)
- The last line of the paragraph and the first line share an analogy, metaphor, or image:

Jeremy grinned at Lynn. Best date ever!

Lynn forced herself to smile back at Jeremy. Worst date ever.

When this connection is missing, the writing can feel disjointed even if each individual paragraph works well on its own.

One useful test is to look at the first and last sentences of adjacent paragraphs. Do they feel connected, or do they seem to belong to different conversations?

Nonfiction: Beauty Through Precision

In nonfiction, beauty often appears as precision.

Readers generally don't expect elaborate language. They are looking for writing that communicates clearly and efficiently while still engaging their attention.

A well-constructed paragraph has its own kind of elegance. It presents an idea, supports it, and moves on without wasting time.

That does not mean nonfiction cannot be vivid. Strong examples, well-chosen details, and clear structure all contribute to readability. If a truly applicable metaphor presents itself, then that adds to the grace.

In today's publishing environment, editors expect manuscripts that are not only accurate but also easily readable. However, if you can use focus, detail, and flow to move beyond mere clean copy, then you stand out from the crowd.

When It Comes Together

At some point in the editing process, you will begin to notice a shift.

The manuscript no longer feels like a collection of parts that need fixing. It starts to feel like a finished piece that needs refinement.

Scenes connect more smoothly. Sentences read more naturally. Details support the larger purpose instead of competing with it.

That is the result of all the earlier work.

Beauty is not something added at the end. It is what emerges when clarity, structure, and purpose align.

You now have the tools to evaluate your manuscript at multiple levels—from overall structure down to individual sentences and details.

There's one thing left to consider, the one most people think about when they think "editing": the copyedit.

Reflection Questions

- Why is clarity essential before a piece of writing can be considered effective or beautiful?
- What does it mean for the elements of a manuscript to be in harmony with each other?
- Why can a well-written sentence still be the wrong choice for a particular scene or paragraph?
- How does selecting the right detail differ from simply adding more description?
- In what ways does consistency of voice contribute to the reader's experience?
- How does the concept of beauty in nonfiction differ from that in fiction?

Exercise

Select a paragraph from your manuscript.

1. Identify:
    - the key idea or purpose of the paragraph
    - the details used to support that idea
    - any sentences that feel decorative rather than necessary
2. Revise the paragraph by:
    - removing or adjusting details that do not support the central purpose
    - ensuring that the tone remains consistent
    - tightening any sentences that interrupt the flow
3. Read the revised paragraph aloud and compare it to the original.
    - Does the paragraph feel more focused?
    - Do the details work together more clearly?

The goal is not to make the paragraph more elaborate, but to make it more cohesive—so that every element contributes to the whole.

CHAPTER NINE

The Copyedit

Have you noticed one thing we've not covered in this book? We've talked about everything from plot structure to sentence metaphors, and yet… What about my typos?

Copyediting is the art of finding typos and simple spelling and grammatical errors. Simple, yet not easy.

Typos Happen

It is a running joke among authors that we can go over a book 40 times in 15 different ways, but the easiest way to find typos is to publish the book. Even professional publishers have this issue. I have a friend who is republishing some books that have been through reprints with three publishers and she's still finding typos! I find errors that I know better than to commit in my published books.

The point I'm making here is that they will happen. Your goal is to mitigate them and catch as many as you can (especially the big or embarrassing ones.) In general, people will forgive forgetting an Oxford comma, especially in fiction, but misspelling a word in nonfiction, especially if it's a word that's part of the vernacular of the topic, can lead to a loss of credibility. Also, some typos can change the meaning of a sentence or be outright embarrassing.

So do your best. Don't skimp on this part. But also, don't beat yourself up if you find an error later.

Seek out Typos

The first most common issue is typos. Granted, spellcheck will catch a lot of these, but you cannot depend on it. Sometimes, the typo creates a word that makes sense in some twisted way. Sometimes, the program just plain misses it. That's why it's always good to use a couple of spellcheck programs in addition to your own eyes.

Some common typos that don't always get noticed:

- a dropped article like "a" or "an"
- a misspelled word that is another word itself. (My foible is *from* and *form*.)
- misuse of an uncommon punctuation
- foreign words that are spelled almost like English ones
- words where a slight change of spelling makes a difference, but the AI can't judge the context, like fiancé vs fiancée. (Fiancé is male; fiancée is female.)
- correct words in the wrong place (For example, in the sentence below, I'd had inevitable instead of inevitably, and spellcheck did not catch it.)

- problems with parallelism (For example, I had a mix of bullet points starting with capitals and small letters, but grammar check did not catch them.)
- made up language and names. It may count them all as misspelled.

It also helps if you know your own bad habits. For example, I inevitably mess up "the." Usually it's *the*, but sometimes, I type the *t* onto the previous word and then the *he*: *I meant he other brother*. Spellcheck did not flag the issue in the sentence, although it signaled "other" as a grammatically questionable choice.

If you know you have issues with particular words, make a list of them so you can check for them in the editing.

Homophones

Another issue that can catch people is mixing up words that sound alike but are spelled differently. For example, *sea* and *see*.

My own crucibles are *discreet* and *discrete*. No matter how often I remind myself and no matter what mnemonic I make, I get confused— and I was a math major. You'd think I'd know if numbers are discreet or discrete, but I can't even tell you now without looking it up!

Like the typos, write down any that you know are a problem to check later. This is also where having a second set of eyes like a beta reader or a good critique partner or group comes in handy.

Changing Verb Tenses

It can be easy to get really involved in a scene— actually feel yourself in it—and start writing in present tense when the book is written in the past. By the same token, since we are used to reading past-tense stories, if you are trying to write present tense, you may find yourself slipping into past—especially if you had just written something that needed to be past tense, like a flashback or someone talking about an earlier event.

This also happens when you are writing overtop an outline or had shorthanded a scene: *Here Vern goes to confront the crook, and he says a spell that knocks Vern on his tail....*

Often, you can catch these in a reread, but if you are concerned (or found several errors), a quick search for some common present- or past-tense verbs can help you uncover errors.

Punctuation Overuse

Have you seen the "theory" going around that you can tell something is AI-written by the use of em-dashes? Ridiculous! I love a good em-dash. However, it does bring a point about overusing a particular punctuation style.

Some punctuation is like "said." They're practically invisible as long as they are used correctly, like commas, periods, and question marks. Exclamation points get noticed. That is the point. However, too many of them in a paragraph or page reads like a hyperactive child, even when the scene is tense.

Em-dashes and parentheses signal interruptions in a conversation. Em-dashes are for emphasis and interruptions that directly relate to the phrase before. Parentheses are for side comments and information separated from the sentence but still important.

Semicolons are not as often used. They indicate a short pause between two sentences, but they should only be used when the sentences are closely tied together.

Forgotten Quote Marks

Quote marks always come in pairs—an open and a close. The one exception is when the person talking says more than one paragraph.

> "The ship is in terrible shape," Lt. Morales told the captain. "Shields at 20% and barely maintaining that. Hull breaches on Decks 14, 17, and 22. Warp drive has overloaded twice, and we've exhausted our quantum cooling reserves. **(No close quote here since she's still talking, but we have an open quote in the next paragraph to show talking is still happening.)**

"On the bright side, we still have torpedoes, and the recreation room reports that the last hit somehow fixed the VR system."

Usually, the close quote gets forgotten. It's a good idea to keep a careful check on the ends of quotes when proofing.

Other things to watch out for.

- In American English, the punctuation always goes inside the quotes unless it changes the meaning of the sentence. (I read "Flowers for Roy.") British English puts punctuation outside except when it's part of the sentence. (I read "Flowers for Roy".)

- Quote marks are used for short works like stories, poems, and songs. Longer works use italics.

- When you have a quote inside a quote, use single quote marks: *"We read 'Ode to Flowers' in class," she said.*

- If using smart quotes (or you're not sure), check that the end quotes face the correct direction. Word especially points them wrong after em-dashes: "—"

Consistency

One of the easiest things to miss—and one of the fastest ways to look unprofessional—is inconsistency.

You may spell a name one way in Chapter One and another way in Chapter Ten. You may capitalize a term sometimes and not others. You may write "email" in one place and "e-mail" in another.

Readers may not always consciously notice, but editors will. In nonfiction, inconsistency can affect credibility. In fiction, it can confuse the reader.

In traditional publishing, it makes an easy excuse for them to reject you. It can also cost you awards.

Watch for:

- character names (especially unusual ones)
- place names
- invented terms or magic systems
- capitalization (e.g., "Captain" vs "captain")
- hyphenation (e.g., "worldbuilding" vs "world-building")

If you have a lot of these, consider keeping a list.

Sometimes, you may make decisions based on style. (For example, I decided in *Space Traipse* not to italicize the names of ships or foreign words.) In that case, you may want to keep a style sheet of decisions you've made so you can apply them consistently. (However, if you are submitting to a publisher, check their preferred style and change accordingly.)

Repeated Words and Phrases

We all have favorite words. They show up quietly and then suddenly appear three times in one paragraph.

Sometimes it's harmless. Sometimes it becomes distracting.

This is especially noticeable with:

- character gestures (shrugged, sighed, nodded)
- intensifiers (very, really, quite)
- descriptive words (dark, small, cold)
- stand-out words (brilliant, just) and profanity

Be especially careful with standout words and profanity. I learned something interesting from best-seller Larry Corriea: Certain words, like profanity, get recorded in the brain three times. That's because when you read, your brain is reading, processing what it just read, and the eyes are moving ahead to what you're about to read. Thus, a word like f**k gets registered not once but thrice for each time it's used. Moral: A little goes a long way.

You don't need to eliminate repetition entirely. Language naturally repeats. Sometimes, you want a word or phrase repeated for parallelism or lyrical flow. What you want to avoid is unintentionally clustering the same word.

A simple search can help you find these patterns.

Missing or Extra Words

These are the errors that make you reread a sentence twice before realizing what's wrong.

Usually spellcheck catches these, but it won't hurt to watch out for them, anyway. Sometimes, you make a mistake that results in a grammatically correct sentence as far as rules are concerned but not meaning.

- missing a small word: She went store.
- doubling a word: He turned turned away.
- skipping part of a phrase because your brain filled it in

These are especially tricky because your brain knows what the sentence should say and reads it that way. That's why techniques like reading slowly, reading aloud, or even reading backward can help catch them. (More on that later!)

Dialogue Formatting

We covered quotation marks, but improper dialogue formatting can create confusion, too.

Be sure you:

- start a new paragraph when a new speaker begins either talking or acting
- keep dialogue and action clearly connected

- have the tags pointing to the person speaking. (My favorite book had a wrong tag and flipped an argument between twins!)

This is less about grammar and more about readability. If a reader has to stop and figure out who is talking, the flow breaks.

Paragraph Length and Breaks

Long paragraphs can be intimidating, even if they are technically correct. Genre also dictates length of paragraphs. Academic and scholarly works allow for longer paragraphs, while more casual reads opt for shorter ones.

Age can be a variable, too. Middle grade and early readers favor shorter paragraphs. They feel less intimidating even when the subject matter is deep.

Look for places where:

- a paragraph shifts focus slightly and could be split
- dialogue is buried inside a large block of text

- nonfiction sections would benefit from clearer visual breaks

Readers scan, especially when reading online or nonfiction. They need visual structure as well as logical structure.

Formatting and Presentation

This is often overlooked but matters, especially for traditional publishing.

Check for:

- consistent indentation or spacing
- consistent use of italics
- consistent chapter headings
- proper formatting for titles of works (italics vs quotation marks)
- that it follows the publisher's guidelines as far as font, margins, etc. if you are submitting

A manuscript that is cleanly formatted signals professionalism before anyone reads a word.

Numbers and Style Choices

In nonfiction especially, how you handle numbers matters.

- Are you writing out numbers (twenty) or using numerals (20)?
- Are you consistent?
- Are units of measurement formatted correctly?

There are rules for numbers that dictate when to use numerals and when to use words. The AP and Chicago Style Guides are good to follow, although different publishers have different style guides. When in doubt, pick a style and stick with it; inconsistency within your manuscript stands out. The Find function makes it easy to spot inconsistencies. Simply search by numeral and by word to make sure you are using each in the correct way.

Copyediting is detail work. It's the part where you slow down and pay attention to the small things that support everything else you've done. It may not be the most exciting stage, but it keeps readers from stumbling over your work.

If grammar and spelling are not your forte, I highly recommend taking a grammar class or getting a good book. Also, Google is your friend when asking questions, but of course, the key is knowing what you don't know. Otherwise, finding a crit group or hiring a proofreader once you are done with the major edits can save you a lot of headaches.

We have a lot to look at now. In the next section, we will bring these elements together into a practical process. I'll tell you my steps for editing and what I look for in each one.

Reflection Questions

> - Why is it important to accept that typos will happen while still taking copyediting seriously?
> - What types of errors are most likely to slip past spellcheck programs?
> - Why are homophones particularly difficult to catch during editing?
> - How can shifting verb tense unintentionally affect a scene?
> - What effect does overusing punctuation (such as exclamation points or em-dashes) have on the reader?
> - Why is consistency in spelling, capitalization, and formatting important for both fiction and nonfiction?
> - How do small errors, such as missing or repeated words, affect readability even when the meaning is clear?
> - Why might copyediting be especially important for nonfiction credibility?

Exercise

1. Start a document. It can be a spreadsheet
    or a list on your computer or even on a
    piece of paper by your desk. You decide
    where is handiest. On this start noting:
    - What words do you usually mistype?
    - What words do you often misspell?
    - What words do you confuse or get
      wrong?
    - What words do you capitalize wrong
      or add a hyphen to that you don't
      need?

    Refer to this list when editing. (You'll see how
    in the next chapter.)

2. Create a second list that is specific to your
    book. In it note names of places,
    characters, or objects with spellings that
    your spellcheck may not recognize.

    Either use this list as you edit to be sure
    you correct flagged words to the spelling
    you want, or add these words to your
    program's dictionary.

CHAPTER TEN

The Six-Step Process

Up to this point, we have talked about the important things to look for when editing. You have examined the heart of your book, shaped its structure, tightened pacing, clarified sentences, and refined how those sentences work together. We discussed grammar and spelling errors to catch in the copyedit.

That is a lot to hold in your head at once.

If you try to fix everything in a single pass, you will miss things. You will also wear yourself out because your brain has to switch between different kinds of decisions—large structural choices, sentence-level adjustments, and tiny mechanical corrections.

That's not necessarily an issue when dealing with a short article, but in the face of a 120,000-word book, it can get intimidating.

That's why we're going to break the editing into steps, each with its own set of goals and a different process. You won't just be reading over and over, so your eyes and your brain will see the manuscript fresh each time.

Why a System Matters

Editing is not just about skill. It is also about process.

When you approach a manuscript without a clear plan, it's easy to:

- fix a sentence
- notice a structural issue
- jump ahead to check something else
- return to the original paragraph without finishing the thought
- assume you checked an issue through out when you only caught the one instance you happened to notice

The result is uneven progress.

A system reduces that friction. It gives you a sequence to follow so that each pass has a clear purpose.

What About Critique Groups and Beta Readers?

I am a big fan of crit groups and beta readers. They inevitably catch things I don't—from the typo or missed word to the fact that my main character does not come off as amazing as I think he is. I credit the Catholic Writers' Guild SFF crit group for the successes of most of my novels, and I hardly ever publish a book before someone else has gone through it.

Having someone else read your manuscript lets you tap into the experience of someone who does not know the story as intimately as you. They not only give you a reader's perspective but will also see things you may not catch because you are so certain it's in there that your brain will fill in the blanks.

I'll be writing a book on critique groups (mostly on how to give good crits). For the purpose of this book, I suggest finding someone with some writing experience or who is very well read in your genre and who will be straight about what does and does not work. It may help your confidence to have someone say they love your writing, but that does not make the story better.

If you can't find a group or a beta reader, there are places to hire one. Fiverr has beta readers, for example.

When to do this in the editing process is a matter of personal choice, but I suggest critiques during the writing process, so provide a clean copy but not a full edit. Beta readers are best when you have a near-finished version.

Deciding What Feedback to Use

Once you involve other readers, you will receive suggestions. Some will be obvious improvements. Others may not fit your intent.

You are not obligated to accept every suggestion you get. You don't even need to accept any of them. It's in your best interest, however, to at least consider them.

Look for patterns:

- If multiple readers are confused at the same point, something needs clarification.
- If several people lose interest in the same section, pacing may be an issue.
- If someone knows grammar better than you, pay attention to their corrections. (At least look up the rules.)

Single comments may indicate personal preference. Repeated comments are usually signals. Even so, you don't have to take their suggestion. You should, however, address the issues. You may come up with an even better idea.

Before You Begin

I don't know about you, but as soon as I finish a story, I'm ready to go back through it again. I've fallen in love with my characters or the topic (and, let's be honest, my own words), and I want to experience them all over again. It's probably the worst time to edit.

Editing works best when you can distance yourself from your work and look at it with a cool, calculating eye. Maybe even hate it a little, but only in the sense that you can see how it can be so much better.

So if you can, I suggest letting the manuscript rest, even if only for a day.

Go write something else. Or read. Or clean house.

And for goodness's sake—*celebrate*! You finished the story!

The Six Steps

I have developed a Six-step process. Each pass builds on the one before it. By the time you reach the final stage, you are no longer making large changes. You are refining what is already working.

These are the steps.

1. Run the spelling and grammar check.

2. Use Find and Replace to fix common problems.
3. Read it through on the computer (or better—have the computer read to you.)
4. Print and read it out loud yourself.
5. Read it backwards (preferably in print rather than on the computer)
6. Run another spelling/grammar check.

Step One: Spellcheck

You do this first just to get the nits out of the way so that you have a cleaner manuscript to work with. After all, it's hard to concentrate on the rise and fall of your pirate adventure when you keep noticing you spelled "barnacle "with two arrs. (See what I did there?)

Nearly every word processor has a spell and grammar check. They vary in quality. I use Word and am not impressed with its grammar check. Grammarly, on the other hand, is rather good, but does not understand author voice and makes a ton of suggestions I'd never follow.

This, of course, is key: Don't blindly trust the machine with its suggestions. It does not understand intent or individuality and may make suggestions that hurt your readability and style. This is especially true in dialogue.

Spellcheck also does not recognize your unique vocabulary (character names, places, objects) unless you teach it. This is why it's important to keep a list of these words.

If you're like me, you may have an alien word that went through more than one spelling. Therefore, the first time spellcheck flags that word, be sure that's the spelling you want before you tell it to Ignore All.

The same thing goes for your style guide.

Another nice thing some spellchecks do is analyze your prose for readability. On Word, that's under Document Insights, or it shows up after you've completed grammar and spell check.

Readability Statistics   ?   ✕

Counts
  Words   30,659
  Characters   150,332
  Paragraphs   1,559
  Sentences   2,268
Averages
  Sentences per Paragraph   1.9
  Words per Sentence   12.5
  Characters per Word   4.6
Readability
  Flesch Reading Ease   67.2
  Flesch-Kincaid Grade Level   6.9
  Passive Sentences   5.5%

                                          OK

You can use this to get a feel for how well you are reaching your audience. The average reading level in the U.S. is between 7th and 8th grade. However, if you are writing a children's book, you'll want to match the grade level, while if you're writing for academia, you probably want to go higher.

I suggest running your story through two different spellcheck programs.

Step Two: Use Find to Catch Troubled Areas

This is where you make use of the list you made in the exercise of your common typos or other nit issues. Go to the Find function and search for those. For example, I'll search for "form" to make sure I use it when I mean form rather than flubbing the word "from." In Word, I can look under Results and scan the sentences there instead of scrolling through the entire document.

Find also makes it easy to catch passive voice. Simply do a search for is was, were, be, and been.

Find and Replace is another great shortcut. Say you alternated between typing your em-dash as " – " and as "—". You can use Replace to switch them out all at once.

This is useful, too, when you are working from different documents from different ages or word processing programs. Sometimes, I have a document that did not use "smart" quotes for example. Smart quotes are curly, while "dumb" quotes are straight. Find and Replace quickly makes them all smart.

Regardless of where you put this step, keep this trick in mind for when you see errors that you know happen more than once in your document.

Read-Throughs on the Computer

The next two steps are where you ask the biggest questions.

- What is the book about?
- Which scenes or sections belong?
- Does the story build toward its key moments?
- Do turning points occur where they should?
- Does the pacing rise and fall in a way that keeps the reader engaged?

We've already discussed what to look for. These reads tell you how to do it.

Step Three: Computer Read-Through

Start by saving this file as a new version: Draft 1, Draft Step 2—whatever helps you keep track. That way, if you make changes you don't like, you have the previous version available.

Before you use a lot of paper, do a read-through on the computer. Start at the beginning and read through to the end. As you do, pay attention to yourself as a reader.

- Where are you excited to turn the page?
- Where are you bored?
- Where are you confused?
- Are you following the plot as it reads or is your brain filling in the blanks?
- Are you falling in love with the subplot rather than the main plot?
- Can you follow the dialogue?

Recently, read-aloud features have gotten surprisingly good. They don't have the same expression as human voice and they mispronounce words (especially homographs like live (liv) and live (liev)) but the one advantage they have over human voice is they read each word exactly as written.

That means that if you wrote a word twice, it will read it twice. If you missed a word, it will not say it. If you use the same word multiple times in a paragraph or page, you will hear it.

Most also highlight the individual word as it reads it. Thus, if you watch your screen as each word is said, you will inevitably notice not just the word but what's around the word. I catch a lot of grammar errors that even grammar checks miss.

In general, I suggest making easy changes as you go and take notes on major issues—the subplot is too long here, the character dialogue too unemotional there. Use a separate notebook or use the comments feature on your computer, whichever works best for you.

Now go through and make all the changes. Use the machete on the bulky scenes. Kill your darlings. Tighten prose. Build description. Whatever it is you thought you needed. If you do a lot of rewriting, run it through spellcheck again to clear up most of the errors.

Then save it.

Step Four: Print and Read Aloud

Now, we gotta use some trees. You'll want to print your manuscript.

Step 1: Once again, open your document and save it under a new version: *draft 2, draft printed*—whatever.

Step 2: If you have any comments in the margins, get rid of them! Fix the issue, reject, accept. If you have comments in the margins when you print, it condenses the page and the print is tiny. Even if your eyes can handle it, it will be harder to see the errors of punctuation.

Step 3: Change the font. You've been looking at these words in the same font for a long time. Changing the font makes your eyes pay attention to the words. Some authors insist comic sans is best for this step. You might also try a different serif; for example, if you type in Calibri, you might want to use a serif font like Georgia. Don't get fancy. Pick something easy to read but different.

Step 4: Make sure the pages are numbered! Use the page number function in the header or footer. If you drop the manuscript or the cat knocks it off the table, you'll be glad you did this.

Step 5: Print the manuscript.

Step 6: Find your red pen and your yellow marker, and start analyzing.

If you are concerned about sentence or paragraph variation, start by looking at the individual page as a whole. Your eyes will tell you if there are too many one- and two-line paragraphs, or paragraphs that take up most of the page.

Now, you read the manuscript again. Why? Because something about reading on paper is different from reading on the computer. Studies have shown that reading online encourages multitasking and distracted reading, a different speed of reading, less retention, and more eye strain. This affects your editing ability. Plus, just like changing the font, moving from computer to print forces you to see the words in a new way.

I recommend reading aloud as well— especially if you have someone you can read to. AI voice is good for what it can do, but your voice, especially knowing your characters, changes the dynamic. Unlike AI, you will trip over an awkward sentence. A badly worded sentence will sound wrong to your ears. Your pace will speed up and slow down, and your emotions will come through. All this lets you evaluate the flow and pace of your story.

It is also where you begin to notice patterns in your writing. Certain words may appear more often than you realize. Sentence structures may repeat. Adjusting these patterns improves readability without changing your voice.

If you start seeing an overused word, make a note to go use Find and replace them with synonyms or revised sentences.

Reading aloud to others is great. I used to read my books to my kids. They found things I didn't, like when my thirdborn realized I had too many minions. It also kept me from getting so swept up in the story that I stopped reading aloud or stopped listening to myself, which does happen when I read aloud alone.

Use your red pen (or purple pen or blue—any color that stands out) to mark errors, make comments, add or slash prose. Don't feel discouraged if you find yourself making a lot of changes even after all the work you'd already done.

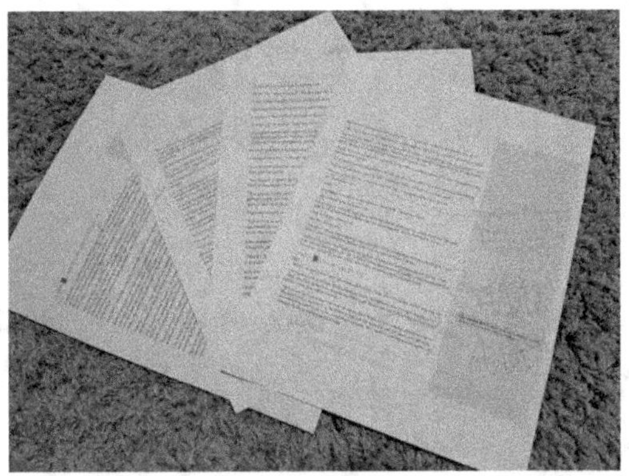

Gapman edits, even after multiple pass-throughs. Notice that I didn't remove the comments. Learn from my mistakes!

Sometimes at this stage, I come up with a scene or a great idea for a rewrite. My margins get crowded and arrows go flying as I note that this paragraph goes here, that one there. I may even need to get notebook paper to write out something and stuff it in. It's exciting!

Once you've finished, you have two choices. If the manuscript is a hot mess of red ink, go back and put in all the edits, save it, and print it again.

If you don't have a lot of changes, then move on to the next step.

Optional: Ripping it Up and Putting it Back Scene by Scene

If you find that your story is truly tangled and disoriented, you may need to do major surgery. This is another time when having it in print can help.

Cut the pages up into scenes and staple the pages together. Write a one-sentence summary on the top page. Then you can more easily reorganize them. This is a process I mentioned from *Bird by Bird* by Anne Lammot, although I've altered it here. I also know other authors who have used this method.

I know some writers use Scrivener or similar programs that let you write individual scenes or chapters then knit them together into a complete novel, so if that works better for you, go ahead!

Step Five: Read it Backward

I learned this trick in high school, and it's been the best editing advice I've ever gotten.

When we read a story, we activate our imagination. We hear it, see it, feel it. As a result, we are looking at a whole story, scene, or action rather than the individual sentences that give it to us.

By reading the story backward, one sentence at a time, you divorce yourself from the flow of the story. Thus, you can see each sentence as its own self.

This is where you:

- find more grammatical errors
- spot passive voice and filler words
- recognize distancing language (seems, appears to)
- work on clarity
- evaluate sentences for their individual beauty

Once again, when you are done, you'll go back to the computer, put in all the edits, and save. This is where a yellow marker comes in handy, as you can highlight each change as you make it and thus not miss any.

Step Six: Final Spellcheck

This step is much like the first: Run your spellcheck and grammar check to catch any new errors that might have come up during the revisions. If you made a lot of changes or have some major edits, you might want to repeat some of the other steps as well.

In fact, if after the final spellcheck, you can put the manuscript aside for a while, I highly recommend doing so, then doing another read-through on the computer at least.

Nonfiction: Same Process, Different Pressure

When I'm working on nonfiction, especially for publication, the process is similar but quicker.

I may combine steps because I have a tighter deadline, am working from an approved outline, or am dealing with a straightforward topic that does not call for especially beautiful language. In those cases, I'm more selective in what I'm looking for: clarity of thought, variation in sentence and paragraphs, and that my examples and quotes truly support the topic.

Copyedit matters even more with nonfiction, IMHO. A typo in a technical term or a misused word can be embarrassing for the magazine or damage credibility.

Naturally, if you have a longer work and have time, I suggest following all the steps. However, if you are on a tight schedule, concentrate on the read-aloud and the backward read (after spellcheck, of course.)

Drafting is exploration. Editing is decision.

You decide what stays. What goes. What gets moved. What gets clarified. You decide what the reader will see—and what they won't.

That's not a small task, but it is a satisfying one.

Even if you still find a typo after publication.

Reflection Questions

- ➢ Why is it useful to begin with a read-through instead of immediately fixing sentences?
- ➢ How does moving sections improve a manuscript?
- ➢ Why is reading aloud an effective editing tool?
- ➢ What advantages do targeted searches offer compared to a standard read-through?
- ➢ How does the editing process change when working with nonfiction under publication constraints?
- ➢ Why is it helpful to separate editing into different passes rather than trying to fix everything at once?
- ➢ How does this system support the idea of gaining distance from your manuscript?

Exercise

No exercise. Go edit!

CHAPTER ELEVEN

Knowing When You're Done

There comes a point in every manuscript when the question shifts from "What needs fixing?" to "Is this ready for submission?"

Sometimes, that question is harder to answer than it sounds. I've known people who have submitted or published their books after a first pass and done quite well. I know others who have revised their books five, ten, fifteen times and still aren't satisfied.

Even with my system, I've skipped steps or have gone through the whole process multiple times, even after crit groups and beta readers.

Knowing when the edit stops improving the manuscript and starts circling it takes skill. It can also take confidence.

The Myth of "Perfect"

The first thing to understand is that there is no such thing as a perfect manuscript.

If you keep looking, you will always find something to change:

- a word that could be stronger
- a sentence that could be rearranged
- a paragraph that could be tighter
- even a subplot that could be strengthened

That does not mean the manuscript is not ready, however.

The goal is not perfection, but a manuscript that works—clearly, consistently, and without distracting errors. That kind of manuscript lets your story reach your reader's heart.

Know what else reaches a reader's heart? A published story—and that can't happen if you are in endless rewrites seeking perfection.

You already know from experience that even published books contain typos. You may have read stories where the character felt weak or the plot wandered more than you liked. Even so, you may have enjoyed the story overall.

Just like you forgive another author for not being perfect, you need to give yourself permission to be good enough. Like my friend, Margaret Gartlgruber, says, "Perfection is the enemy of done."

Signs the Manuscript Is Working

Instead of asking whether the manuscript is flawless, ask whether it is functioning the way it should.

- Does the story or argument hold together from beginning to end?
- Do scenes and sections support the central purpose?
- Does the pacing feel natural rather than forced?
- Are the sentences clear and direct?

- Do the details support rather than distract?

If the answer to these questions is yes, you are close if not already there.

At this stage, most remaining changes are small refinements rather than structural fixes.

When You Start Making Sideways Changes

One of the clearest signs that you are nearing the end is that your edits stop improving the manuscript in a meaningful way.

You may find yourself:
- swapping one word for another and then changing it back
- rearranging sentences without improving clarity
- adjusting phrasing simply because you have seen it too many times
- rewriting because you came up with one more idea

These are not necessarily bad instincts. They are signs that the manuscript is stable. However, if you are at the point where you are no longer fixing problems so much as revisiting decisions, it's probably time to let go.

Nonfiction and Perfection

One nice thing about nonfiction is it's more often done on assignment and deadline, and may not feel as personal as fiction. Even so, it's easier, I think, to worry about perfection in nonfiction. A small ambiguity in fiction may be interpreted as nuance. In nonfiction, it can affect whether someone gets your point.

When you reach the final stage in nonfiction, of course, you need to pay particular attention to factual accuracy, consistency of explanation, and details of spelling in names, correct dates, etc. However, when you start rewriting arguments or chains of logic trying to squeeze one more iota of persuasion or are concerned about one more kind of reader you want to reach, you may need to declare victory and move on.

The Risk of Over-Editing

It is possible to edit the life out of a manuscript.

This usually happens when you begin smoothing every sentence to the point where the voice loses its distinctiveness.

You have already worked to sharpen your writing without dulling your voice. At this stage, that balance matters even more.

If a sentence is clear, effective, and consistent with the tone of the piece, it does not need to be rewritten simply because it could be different.

This can be a danger, too, when doing your final spelling/grammar check. Remember that in addition to pure grammar rules-following, most spelling and grammar checks suggest "improvements" based on the common language that it learned from, which generally means the Internet: marketing, websites, and every clickbait article ever published. Don't lose your uniqueness to the crowdthink.

A Practical Test

One of the simplest ways to judge whether you are done is to step back and read a section without stopping.

If you can read it as a reader rather than an editor—without feeling the need to fix something every few lines—that is a good sign.

You may still notice small issues. That is normal.

The question is whether those issues interfere with the reading experience.

When Do You Need a Professional

I'll be honest: I "grew up" as a writer in the world of small presses and magazines, so I've worked with a wide variety of editors. Some were excellent. Others were so bad that I demanded to take back my manuscript to fix the errors they put in. Some didn't just make corrections, but told me why, thus teaching me.

As a result, I seldom hire a professional editor for my books because I feel confident in my ability to do the job.

That said, I am a fan of professional editors. I'm now writing a middle grade SF series for Pauline Press and am blessed to be working with some fantastic editors. Their suggestions are making the story so much better (and this is after my excellent crit group had worked it through.)

Professional editors are not cheap, and they shouldn't be. They will guide you through a lot of the steps we've outlined in this book, but they do it from years, even decades of experience and probably some formal training as well. This lets them see what works and why.

So, when do you need a professional? That's an independent choice. However, here are some questions to consider:

- How strong is my command of written English?
- How well do I understand what makes a good story, especially one in my genre?
- Is this my first novel?

- Am I self-publishing or aiming for one of the Big Five traditional publishers and want an edge?
- Have I been through crit groups and beta readers and still feel my book is not right but can't pinpoint what's wrong?

There are different kinds of editors, from developmental, who look at the big picture issues of plot and characterization, to copy editors and proofreaders. It's beyond the scope of this book to define them, and many will do more than one type. When selecting an editor, be sure you know what they will do and how much they charge. Also ask:

- what experience they have in your genre
- what other books they've edited (then find them on Amazon and check their quality and sales)

Before you give an editor your manuscript, do your best to edit it. That cuts down on their work and lets them concentrate on the things you could not find, ensuring you get more for your money.

Letting the Manuscript Go

At some point, you send the manuscript out. If you are sending it to a publisher or an agent, most likely they will have their own editorial comments for you to consider—another argument for not worrying about perfection.

If you are self-publishing, then you have complete control. That means if you find that sneaky typo that escaped notice for the 40+ passes before you loaded it onto Amazon or whatever publishing platform you use, then all you need to do is fix it and reload the corrected copy. Annoying, but easy.

Even so, letting go may feel a little like sending your kid to college. You will always feel like there was one more thing to say, one more thing you're sure you missed.

That's okay, but remember books, like kids, are meant to leave our grasp. That's the only way they can enrich the world.

But that only happens once you let go.

You wrote this book because you wanted to make the world better. Maybe it's with advice.

Maybe important information. Maybe you just want to entertain, to give readers a happy escape for a few hours. Those are all worthy goals.

I wrote this book with the intention of helping you to achieve your goal so that you can celebrate that wonderful new book. So edit! Wield that machete with confidence! Be bold. Be critical. Enjoy the process and take everything you learn with you to the next project.

Because there is always a next project.

Reflection Questions

> - Why is it more useful to think in terms of a manuscript "working" rather than being "perfect"?
> - What are some signs that editing has shifted from meaningful improvement to minor adjustment?
> - Why is it difficult to maintain objectivity after multiple editing passes?
> - When is the right time to hire a professional editor?
> - Why is clarity especially important when deciding a nonfiction manuscript is ready?
> - What are the risks of continuing to revise a manuscript beyond the point where major issues have been addressed?

Exercise

Choose a chapter or section of your manuscript.

1. Read it straight through without stopping to edit.
2. After reading, write down:
    - where your attention dropped
    - where you felt confused
    - where the writing felt strong
3. Make only the changes that clearly improve clarity or flow.

Leave everything else alone.

This exercise helps you practice recognizing the difference between necessary edits and optional ones—an essential skill in deciding when a manuscript is ready to move on.

The Write Boost

Practical Writing and Marketing Guides for Growing Writers

The Write Boost: Practical Writing and Marketing Guides for Growing Writers is a series of short, focused eBooks designed to help beginning and early-intermediate writers strengthen their writing craft and build real momentum. Each volume tackles one essential skill—from worldbuilding to editing, goal-setting to critique groups, idea generation to author marketing—with clear instruction, real examples, and practical exercises you can use right away.

Written by award-winning author Karina Fabian, these guides combine decades of professional experience, honest lessons learned, and a healthy dose of encouragement. You don't have to master everything at once. Just pick the boost you need, apply it, and keep moving forward.

KEEP IN TOUCH

If you want to learn about future books, please
- Sign up for my newsletter. https://fabianspace.substack.com/subscribe Get short stories, updates, and a free book!
- Visit my website at https://karinafabian.com
- Follow me on Facebook: https://www.facebook.com/Karina-Fabian-Speculative-Fiction-with-a-Grin-2233839790277963

ABOUT THE AUTHOR

Karina Fabian is an award-winning novelist, speaker, and stand-up comedian who has spent decades telling stories in as many ways as she can manage, from space-faring nuns to dragon private investigators. She's written over 50 science fiction and fantasy novels, plus short stories and humorous works.

In addition to writing fiction, she teaches workshops and webinars for beginning writers, sharing the lessons she's learned through success, trial and error, and stubborn perseverance. She believes you can take the craft seriously without taking yourself too seriously—and that writing is at its best when skill, heart, and a little bit of laughter work together.

Karina lives on Merritt Island with her husband, two of her four kids, two dogs, and a menagerie of imaginary friends who all want to tell her their stories.

THERE'S MORE FUN IN FABIANSPACE!

Science Fiction

<u>Space Traipse: Hold My Beer</u>: Redneck ingenuity and common sense in a Star Trek-ish universe. Enjoy the adventures of the *HMB Impulsive*.

<u>The Rescue Sisters</u>: Intrepid women doing dangerous missions in space for the love of God and humankind.

<u>The Old Man and the Void</u>: Dex hunts relics on the edge of the black hole, and bags the catch of a lifetime.

<u>Jovian Heat</u>: As the next Great Storm of Jupiter rises, Cass must find the father of a baby in peril—but the father died before the child was conceived.

Fantasy

<u>DragonEye Story</u>: Vern's a snarky dragon on the wrong side of the Interdimensional Gap, solving crimes, battling evil, and saving the universes on an all-too-regular basis.

<u>Madness of Kanaan</u>: Deryl isn't crazy; he's psychic, and aliens of two worlds thinks he can save them. Maybe he can—but can he regain his sanity in the process?

Horror

<u>Neeta Lyffe, Zombie Exterminator</u>: Neeta's an average exterminator, taking out bugs, rodents, and the undead. Can she keep her friends alive, pay her bills, and find romance?

<u>Frightliner and Other Tales of the Supernatural (with Colleen Drippé)</u>: Truck-driving vampires terrorizing the road, Southern women doing what needs doing, a zombie wedding—a great story collection for horror lovers.

A Puzzle in a Tunnel: Autistic Conservative Rebels on the Right